Participation and the pursuit of equality

Essays in adult learning, widening participation and achievement

Edited by
Alan Tuckett

A festschrift for Veronica McGivney

niace
promoting adult learning

© 2007 National Institute of Adult Continuing Education
(England and Wales)

21 De Montfort Street
Leicester
LE1 7GE

Company registration no. 2603322
Charity registration no. 1002775

NIACE has a broad remit to promote lifelong learning opportunities for adults.
NIACE works to develop increased participation in education and training,
particularly for those who do not have easy access because of class, gender,
age, race, language and culture, learning difficulties or disabilities,
or insufficient financial resources.

You can find NIACE online at www.niace.org.uk

Cataloguing in Publication Data
A CIP record of this title is available from the British Library

Designed and typeset by Avon DataSet Ltd, Bidford-on-Avon, Warwickshire
Printed and bound in the UK by Ashford Colour Press, Gosport

ISBN: 978 1 86201 256 1

Contents

Contributors

John Field
Deputy Principal, University of Stirling

Wilma Fraser
Senior Lecturer in the Dept of Post-Compulsory Education and Training at Canterbury Christ Church University and Programme Director for the MA in Lifelong Education and Professional Practice

Ursula Howard
Director, NRDC and Head of the Bedford Group for Lifecourse and Statistical Studies

Peter Lavender
Director for Research, Development and Information, NIACE

Stephen McNair
Director, Centre for Research into the Older Workforce

Julia Preece
Centre for Research and Development in Adult and Lifelong Learning (CRADALL), University of Glasgow

Chris Scarlett
Writer and researcher

Maria Slowey
Vice-President for Learning Innovation and Registrar

Judith Summers
Consultant and writer and Honorary Research Fellow of NIACE. She was a member of the Kennedy Committee on Widening Participation

Richard Taylor
Director of Continuing Education and Lifelong Learning, University of Cambridge

Jane Thompson
Principal Research Officer, NIACE

Alan Tuckett
Director, NIACE

Annie Winner
Left the WEA in July 2006 and is now working freelance

Chapter 1

Participation and the pursuit of equality

Alan Tuckett

This collection of essays was conceived and commissioned as a *festschrift* – a testament to the range of interests and achievements of Veronica McGivney, on her retirement as Principal Research Officer of the National Institute of Adult Continuing Education. Each of the contributors was happy to share in the public recognition of the importance of Veronica's contribution to the interests of adult learners, and to demonstrate the continuing importance of the questions addressed in her work. The collection looks back to the lessons that can be drawn from two decades and more of struggles to secure greater equity for marginalised groups, and forward to the social, political and educational policy challenges facing providers, administrators, politicians and public alike in securing life-wide and life-long learning for all. I am grateful to Jane Thompson and Peter Lavender for their help in commissioning pieces, and to Charlotte Owen and Virman Man for their perseverance and professionalism in seeing the volume through to publication.

I met Veronica first at the Friends Centre, one of a tiny number of student managed voluntary adult education centres, based in the Quaker meeting house in the Lanes in Brighton. I was a new Principal and she came to teach a course in European Studies, sponsored by the University of Sussex Centre for Continuing Education. She was then, as now, meticulously prepared, generous with her time, and above all authoritative and fun. After university at Exeter, where another distinguished adult educator, Juliet McCaffery, was a student friend, she taught European languages in secondary schools and adult education centres. She was a lecturer in literature at the University of Nairobi; tutor and tutor-counsellor at the Open University; tutor in the School of European Studies and the Centre for Continuing Education at the University of Sussex; and Research Fellow at the Sussex European Research Centre based at the University of Sussex. She joined the National Institute of Adult Continuing Education in the mid 1980s, and retired from her post as Principal Research Officer in 2005. Her work enjoys both national and international recognition, and she played a full part in conferences in the UK and abroad.

At NIACE, Veronica co-ordinated International Women's Day events, led the research support unit, and conducted a wide range of in-depth, qualitative studies on many aspects of adult learning as well as a number of evaluations of practice and provision for NIACE's many constituents. These included local education authorities, universities, adult and community education providers, REPLAN, UDACE, the ESRC, the former Departments of Employment and of Education and Employment, the European Social Fund, the Pre-School Learning Alliance, the Oxfordshire Strategic Partnership, NIACE Cymru, the British Council and Coventry Economic Development Unit.

As John Field shows in his chapter in this book, few reports of academic research in the field of adult education have had the policy impact of Veronica's 1990 study, *Education's for Other People*. The book reported on the findings of research Veronica had undertaken, with support from the Economic and Social Research Council, on adult participation in education. The work was done at a time of rapid change, as new legislation, the Education Reform Act of 1988, was being introduced, when the bastion of adult learning provision, the Inner London Education Authority, was being closed down, and when a major expansion in higher education, designed for young people, was being taken up in increasing numbers by adults. As Veronica reflected a decade later:

> The study revealed persisting class, age and occupational divisions between participants and non-participants in organised learning. It also showed that there were wide variations between further and higher education institutions, local education authorities and other providers in the extent and nature of the efforts they were making to attract and work with the sizeable groups who were not taking advantage of organised learning opportunities. (McGivney, 2001, p. 1)

A formidable collection of barriers – practical, financial and attitudinal –

stood in the way of many of the groups under-represented in the system. Whilst the study showed that some institutions had developed effective strategies for engaging neglected groups, there was a widespread belief in the majority of institutions that since programmes were open to all, the onus was on individuals to take advantage of them, and strong resistance to suggestions that institutional practices should be adapted better to serve working-class people, black communities or people with disabilities. Taken with the sequence of quantitative studies led by Naomi Sargant, the work instigated by *Education's for Other People* made a convincing case for adult educators to address two questions – 'who isn't there?' and 'what can be done about it?'

Within a decade of the study, political parties across the spectrum recognised the economic and social justice case for addressing how to widen participation and achievement, and many institutions recognised the need to examine their own practices to that end. A national participation target was adopted, and government policy enshrined a commitment to lifelong learning for social inclusion as well as economic modernisation. And if, as she reported later, there was a return to more utilitarian concerns in policy after the turn of the millennium, there was, nevertheless, a sea-change in the understanding of the issues involved in securing successful participation.

In this and in a formidable range of successor qualitative studies, Veronica fleshed out the experiences of under-represented groups in seeking access to post-compulsory education, and what institutions could do to make provision accessible and a positive experience for second-chance learners. The titles of her studies paint a clear view of her analysis of the issues involved: in 1992 she published *Motivating Unemployed Adults to Undertake Education and Training*; in 1993 *Women in Education and Training: Barriers to Access, Informal Starting Points and Progression Routes*; in 1994 *Wasted Potential: Training, and Career Progression for Part-Time and Temporary Workers*. By 1996 she had moved on to the issues of student retention, which showed an absolute divide between institutions which recorded student withdrawal by listing institutional barriers as the reasons listed, and those which located withdrawal by cataloguing the ways students failed to adapt effectively to institutions. Few integrated both approaches. In 1999 she published *Excluded Men* and a major literature review on *Informal Learning* – a theme returned to strongly in this book, in Ursula Howard's chapter 'Sides to middle'. *Recovering Outreach*, published in 2000, addressed an absence in the policy memory of policy-makers and planners – highlighting the wealth of practice that demonstrated that for adult learning, the curriculum begins with learner engagement, not with the first meeting of a structured class. Later studies look at achievement and progression routes in adult learning, the impact of gender on participation, the nature of achievement, and she wrote, too, on curricular studies.

In addition to books looking at issues with national policy implications, Veronica undertook a number of detailed local and institutional studies. Her evaluation of the Women's Education Project in Belfast highlighted the energy and social transformation that feminist education strategies engendered, and her study of the way parents used pre-schools as a springboard for their own education journeys made the point powerfully that no one goes to a pre-school for themselves. They go to enrich the experience and extend the social contacts of their children. But they stay for themselves. Her pre-school study helped to inform the surge in family learning provision, and provided evidence of the diverse and complex learning journeys adults undertake.

Veronica was always an exacting and inspiring colleague. She set high standards for herself, was generous with her time, contributed enormously to the induction and development of younger researchers and made invaluable contributions to NIACE's strategic thinking across the years. Her humour and wry commentary on so much that has become ridiculous about pragmatic policy making and implementation acted as a very necessary and continuing reminder of the personal principles that always underpinned her contribution to adult learning.

All in all, as the bibliography at the end of this book demonstrates, Veronica's contribution to our understanding of adult learners, their purposes in learning, and the journeys they undertake has made an unparalleled contribution to informing policy debate affecting adult and lifelong learning in England and beyond.

That is reason enough for a volume of celebration. But at a time when a million adults have been displaced from structured provision over a three-year period, it is also important to revisit the questions 'who isn't there?' and 'what is to be done about it?'

Each of the ten chapters in this collection takes a theme in Veronica's work, and explores options for the future in the light of recent history. There are some shared concerns, of course. There is real frustration that the unremitting focus on the formal education of the young should, if anything, have been reinforced over the last decade. New Labour took office with such a generous and inclusive vision of lifelong learning, which makes the subsequent return to a narrow utilitarian focus on learning for work all the more dispiriting. Each contributing author asserts strongly that the pursuit of an inclusive and egalitarian society through inclusive and egalitarian polices for the education of adults is right for a civilised society and for a dynamic economy. Together they represent a powerful and coherent case for the support of adult learning, in Jane Thompson's memorable phrase, 'for a change'.

The opening chapters cover the relationship between informal learning and the pursuit of learning for everyone; the central sequence of chapters addresses women's education, social class and adult learning, older people, learning and work, and the place of volunteers as learners and teachers in their own right; these are followed by two chapters which look at widening participation in further and higher education. The final chapter returns to the key theme of this introduction, evaluating Veronica's work in participation studies, and considering its implications for adult learning and active citizenship.

In the first chapter Ursula Howard opens with three stories that demonstrate how learning touches lives in different ways, and how adults' learning journeys are often circuitous. She argues that everyone organises their learning in different ways, and that we make a profound mistake if we limit our thinking about adult learning solely to structured provision supported by state funding.

Picking up on a recurrent theme in Veronica's writing, Ursula emphasises the importance of informal learning, reflects on the richness of mutual improvement traditions through the nineteenth century, and their progressive marginalisation once state funding is introduced. Her stories, she argues, show that 'adult learning will not collapse if state funding collapses, but that some are crucially helped by strong state support'.

She goes on, 'the stories also bring home the challenges which adult educators face in advocating adult learning in an era when policy priorities again and again put young people before older ones and economic aims before social concerns.' She contrasts this kind of prioritising with the inclusive vision with which Labour articulated its ambitions in 1998. She suggests that this way of setting priorities, the culture of 'hard choices' is a symptom of a deeper malaise in society, a bi-polarity, where tests separate success from failure, ins from outs, and where, characteristically, the oppositions we establish work to create the marginalisation of those adults who benefit least from our structures.

We need, she suggests, a more inclusive approach to the work – seeing the role of educator more as facilitator than distributor of knowledge. She explores this in the context of adult literacy work – arguing that the structures of the English national curriculum framework for Skills for Life need to be articulated with literacy as social practice. She argues, too, for fuzzier boundaries between education, community development and social justice and for an educational practice where the agenda cannot just be given, top-downward, but negotiated collaboratively by all the actors in civil society, where trust and mutuality have as much prominence as monitoring and targets.

She finishes with the metaphor that provides the title for her piece. It is one that works, too, for much of Veronica's work – by giving central attention to the experiences of marginalised groups, we make our world anew.

Veronica McGivney led NIACE's work in women's education for many years. It was, for her, a central and passionate concern – and is reflected here in three chapters. They begin with Jane Thompson's powerful plea for the recovery of feminist perspectives in adult learning debates. Jane highlights the limitations of the narrow labour market focus in current lifelong learning policies, and the consequences of the neo-conservative world view she sees in New Labour policies for women's life chances, given that 'ours is an intellectual and political tradition that...repeatedly consigns questions of sexual inequality and repression to the dustbin of history.' She maps the changing pattern of women's engagement with education and work – the increase in overall participation offset by persistent inequalities in access to power and agency. Continuing occupational segregation, under-valuing of part-time work, and the management of expectations all contribute to the persistent exclusion of women. She contrasts the vision of an inclusive engagement with adult learning of *The Learning Age* with the Government's subsequent practice. It has, she argues, 'consistently and systematically prioritised employability' over social solidarity – seeking behaviour modification from individuals to address problems that are systemic. In a society where women experience continuing high levels of domestic violence, inequality at work, poorer pensions, and exclusion from leadership and decision-making, she argues, the conditions for a learning society are destroyed by plastering over inequalities in political discourse. Time, as her title declares, to use the 'f' word again – to recover feminist perspectives in education, and to reconnect education processes with the wider movement for equality and justice.

In 'Women and education in the South', Julia Preece takes consideration of the inhibitions to gender equity in education arising from globalisation beyond the UK to a global stage. Like Veronica McGivney's work on adult education in emerging economies, and Jane Thompson's chapter in this book, she recognises that education is about 'politics, power, attitudes and behaviour', as much as it is about skills. She considers the scale of the challenge in the Global South where a majority of women continue to lack literacy skills, where 60 per cent of the children between the ages of six and 11 now not in school are girls, where the benefits of access to education can be seen in reduced child mortality rates, lower levels of HIV infection, increased economic independence, and yet where women's education is a low priority or no priority for many nation states. Her analysis of the causes of the current malaise begins with an examination of the way colonial education systems overrode the indigenous pedagogies that embraced lifelong learning principles as foundations for active citizenship and nation-building. She moves on to explore the way the challenging aspirations for women's education identified at the United Nations world conference on women in Beijing, and those adopted in the Dakar commitment to Education for All, were seriously eroded in the eight development targets adopted by the UN as Millennium Development Goals. As Preece recognises, adult education is not a development goal at all. The World Bank and international aid agencies have focused increasingly on the goal of universal primary education to the exclusion of other educational goals – and their concerns are mirrored in national strategies for poverty reduction. Yet as she argues, educated women send their children to school, and provide living examples of the benefits education can bring. She concludes with an exploration of strategies that do work in securing empowerment for women, across Asia and Africa, and illustrates the energies of non-government agencies dedicated to challenging the imbalances.

'A gift in their hands' comes at the same themes through a review of the place and practices of women's education in the Workers' Educational Association. Wilma Fraser, Chris Scarlett and Annie Winner have a clear aim – 'We want the story of women's education in the WEA to speak to those educational and social movements which seem caught up in a cycle of ever-repeating marginalisation and powerlessness.' Writing from a position where the great flowering of women's education in the WEA in the 1970s through to the 1990s had ended, they assert the importance of story-telling as a resource for inspiring new initiatives. Certainly, the story they tell is of two steps forward, one step back as external and internal forces contest the separate space for women's education that has been serially negotiated in the WEA. 'A gift in their hands' begins with the creation of the WEA as the Association to Promote the Higher Education of Working Men, taking in the struggle to secure a name change, the appointment in 1910 of the Association's first women's officer; the expansion of women's roles in public life during the major wars of the century, and the subsequent re-assertion of their domestic duties. But the heart of the essay reviews the flowering of women's studies in the WEA, which benefited from the dynamic cultural impact of the feminist movement of the 1970s, and the way subsequent external funding policies and internal WEA politics influenced, shaped and limited the work. 'The language of empowerment,' they suggest, 'was hijacked by the empty rhetoric of the market place and education's transformative potential began to be harnessed and corralled by the culture of learning outcomes, accreditation, progression routes, and added value'. Their conclusion, that social progress involves struggle and the long haul, with periods of gain followed by 'being pushed back to the borders' is offered as a message of hope to people in social movements experiencing adverse conditions, and, perhaps, reinforces Jane Thompson's argument that the time is surely right for a re-assertion of feminist perspectives in adult education work.

'How can it be that social class has become currently so unfashionable?' Dick Taylor's essay sets out to address this question, and what implications it has for widening participation strategies. He examines the dominant view that social class is now of less empirical importance, and the view, born of the failure of post-war social policy in industrial nations to diminish class differentials in distributive outcomes, that 'welfare socialism' has failed. He argues that class structures have changed, becoming more volatile and complex than at any previous period, and, with Westergaard, that whilst class 'has been re-declared dead', its economic configuration has become even sharper. That all this should be accompanied by the exclusion of class from contemporary social policy debates is the product of the political and ideological stance of New Labour, Dick argues. This has, he suggests, a direct impact on the focus and rationale for widening participation policies in lifelong learning. Like other contributors, Dick is positive about the initial commitments of the Government to lifelong learning. 'One of the most creditable aspects of New Labour's education policy since 1997 has been the advocacy of widening participation,' he argues, and he recognises, too, that policy rhetoric has been backed by resourcing. However, he suggests, optimism about this focus was short-lived as Labour rejected the

emancipatory and democratic focus of Tawney's educational philosophy and
Cardinal Newman's liberalism for a narrow utilitarian and remorselessly
individualist approach to education and skills. Widening participation
becomes an arm of human capital rather than a tool of emancipation. New
Labour has, Taylor argues, 'adopted a wholly individualistic frame of
reference,' and has focused increasingly, in higher and further education
alike, on the needs of 17–21-year-olds, to the detriment of adults. He looks
to the energy of social movements to contest these developments, and offers
two strategic foci for recovering a class-informed and generous lifelong
learning policy, each grounded in a commitment to democratic and
discursive modes of study.

If women's education and empowerment have slipped down the policy
agenda – in part because women's participation across the range of post-
compulsory education has increased – then older people, like working-class
people, continue to be under-represented in participation and policy alike.
Indeed, one in four over-60s have lost places in publicly-funded further
education in a single year, 2005–2006, as a result of radical re-balancing of
funding streams, by a Government increasingly focused on its utilitarian
agenda. Despite demographic change, little of the re-focused resources have
been targeted at the learning needs of older workers, as Stephen McNair
makes clear in his essay, 'The "baby bulge" generation comes to retirement'.
He cites the key conclusion of the Turner Commission's report on pensions,
that there are only three options that flow from the impact of demography on
pensions arrangements in the UK – to be poorer in old age, to save more
throughout life, or to work longer. Stephen concludes that only the third of
these options is politically practicable in the short-run. However, to pursue
that option, it will be necessary to overcome age discrimination among
employers and policy-makers alike. Stephen takes comfort from the pace of
change in areas of the South East, where there is full employment, and where
housing shortages, house prices and overloaded transport systems inhibit
further migration. There, he argues, employers increasingly recognise the
benefits of retaining experienced older workers and recruiting others back to
work. But do older people want to work longer? The findings of three
interlocked studies reported on here, perhaps surprisingly, overwhelmingly
say 'yes'. A large majority of older people feel positive about work, and
express a willingness to stay on at work, so long as they are fit and able, and
as long as opportunities are offered for part-time work. Meeting their needs
will involve the redesign of jobs and working practices, and re-thinking
training priorities, to make the best use of available talent. Stephen concludes
that to do this successfully will involve change in attitudes and practices alike

– for employers and government. 'Even adult educators,' he concludes, 'who have always known from experience the waste and injustice of a "front-end" model of learning' have concentrated their second-chance and return-to-study programmes on adults from their mid-20s to their 40s. Where they have considered the needs of older workers it has been through preparation for retirement courses. The challenge Stephen McNair poses is to adapt such programmes to fit the more complex life and work choices facing the 'baby boomer' generation.

The overwhelming focus of debate about lifelong learning centres on the allocation of public resources, and on the ways publicly-funded professional staff can support widening participation and achievement. Much less attention has been afforded to the contribution volunteers can make, or to their own learning needs. In his essay, Peter Lavender suggests that this is, in part, because our professional discourse is at best uncertain about the additional value volunteers bring, and in particular because of a concern with their motives in volunteering. He points to the coalescence of a range of social policy themes – including 'active citizenship', the responsibility of individuals to care for others, the idea that the State should have responsibility to fill in gaps left by individual, volunteer and voluntary sector support – and their impact on voluntary work and the use of volunteers in a range of statutory contexts. In education this leads to a striking contrast, between the 'self-actualising model of student participation in which the goal of student empowerment' is a common theme, and the absence of any such agency in the engagement of volunteers.

Peter explores the role of volunteers over a 30-year period, starting with an analysis of the central role volunteers played as tutors in the first national literacy campaign, and their exclusion from other activity. There was, he suggests, suspicion of volunteers' motives in volunteering – 'there was unease about motives in general, with the organisers suspicious of altruism and the volunteers unhappy about motives of self-interest. The result was that volunteers were treated as unpaid part-time staff, and were 'rarely required to contribute opinions or decision-making skills'. He shows through examination of youth policy how voluntary work migrated to community service over time, as planners increasingly saw a national community service programme as a practical option to engage 'idle hands' at a time of high unemployment. This was accompanied by a change in the public image of voluntary work from being something altruistic for middle-class people to seeing it as appropriate activity for working-class young people in need of state benefits. He analyses the parallels between the development of these ideas under Thatcherism, and their renaissance under the current Government, and explores how best educators might use volunteers in support of statutory programmes now. His challenge is to recognise volunteers as contributors whose learning needs have every bit as much claim on organisers' support as paid staff, and to see altruism – the 'concern for the common weal of others' – focusing on younger people spill over to other age groups. He suggests we should be ready to make more of a success of it than we have done in the past.

The next two essays turn to strategies for further and higher education better to adapt to meet the needs of under-represented adults.

Learning Works, the report of the Kennedy Committee, appeared on 4 May 1997 – three days after the election of a new Labour government. The Committee was established by the Further Education Funding Council to advise on strategies for widening participation in further education. The report shared many of the perspectives and analyses that had informed Veronica McGivney's work over the previous decade as Judith Summers, a key member of the Committee, recognises in her essay here.

For many in the field *Learning Works* and the 1998 Government Green Paper *The Learning Age* reflected a high-water mark in public recognition of the challenge in improving the quantity and quality of participation by under-represented groups. As Helena Kennedy commented (echoing NIACE's own Tony Uden), the experience of the bulk of the population is that 'if at first you don't succeed, you don't succeed'. The Committee recognised that there was nothing inevitable about this. Providers had in place a wealth of experience that needed to be generalised. It was heady stuff but, as Judith Summers suggests, some of the key recommendations in the report played better with providers than with policy-makers. She focuses in particular on the central proposal to create a 'new learning pathway' – to offer effective support to adult learners in shaping successful journeys through further education. As Judith explains, 'The heart of the proposal was to accredit guidance, tutorial and learning support, so that it could be made properly and coherently available as the 'glue" which bound learning together, and be recognised by the then funding methodology.' The task was to find a mechanism, parallel to but different from Access Courses, which could recognise the importance and value of informal as well as formal progression routes, whilst enabling learners to pursue multiple goals.

Judith provides a spirited case for the proposal, an analysis of its failure to be endorsed in national policy, and rich evidence of the way the ideas are reflected in a variety of local practice. It is not surprising that as this volume appears Government is grappling with the same issues and concerns as it seeks to identify how best to support progression below 'Level 2' – the equivalent of five good GCSEs. Nor is it surprising that the 2005 NIACE enquiry into adult learning in further education colleges shares much of its analysis with the Kennedy report. In a system designed to meet the needs of young people, the interests of adults tend to be shoe-horned in as an afterthought – even where they constitute the great majority of participants.

Maria Slowey's essay examines how far there has been a policy-learning journey over the last 20 years affecting adult learners' access to higher education. For her analysis she draws on her own experience as researcher, contributor to national committees and practitioner, looking first at key messages that emerged from the major 1980s study of adult learners, commissioned by the Department of Education and Science, and published as *Choosing to Learn* (Woodley *et al*, 1987). This highlighted the complexity and diversity of adults' learning journeys, their perseverance and dedication. Maria quotes Veronica McGivney's conclusion that whilst learning journeys may be cumulative they are seldom linear, and the *Choosing to Learn* conclusion that few institutions in the 1980s had a clear focus on adult learning needs. She then asks how far developments over 20 years can offer evidence that policy memory and research affect what happens. The period covered saw almost a doubling of student numbers in the decade and a half to 2001, a major review of higher education chaired by Lord Dearing, the re-organisation of higher education into a sector combining polytechnics and former universities, the emergence of research selectivity exercises and a renewed focus on recruitment of the young.

During this period there was, Maria notes, an absolute and relative increase in the participation rates of women, mature students and part-time students, with less evidence of improvement in participation by working-class students, part-time undergraduates – outside the Open University – or by students with disabilities. She explores measures taken to improve access and their impact on adults in higher education: first the focus on creating a credit accumulation and transfer system, stimulated by the work of the Council for National Academic Awards; second the focus on equal opportunities led by the National Advisory Body; third the Higher Education Quality Council's focus on quality assurance; fourth the impact of Research Assessment

Exercises; and fifth reviews of higher education funding, and in particular the work of the Cubie report.

Time after time, her conclusion is that adults benefit, if at all, accidentally. Whilst *Choosing to Learn* had noted the importance of part-time fee levels, and the lack of support available to part-time learners as key barriers to participation as early as 1987, Cubie in Scotland – and for that matter the 2004 Higher Education White Paper in England – were silent on the issue.

Following substantial pressure, modest measures have been introduced in England, as Maria notes, and since then a major report on the funding of part-time participation in higher education has been commissioned by the Welsh Assembly. Nevertheless, it is hard to escape Maria's conclusion that despite these modest gains policy and resourcing remains focused on extending initial education (schooling) for young people as opposed to supporting the learning needs of a broader population through recurrent education (in 1970s terminology), continuing education (1980s) or lifelong learning (1990s). Indeed, the gap she points to, between policy aspirations and practice on the ground, is a common theme wherever we look at lifelong learning policy.

John Field's chapter returns to the impact of *Education's for Other People* and the wider contribution Veronica has made to participation studies in the UK and the wider international research community. He recognises the importance of national overview studies, both quantitative and qualitative, in providing a framework for the myriad local studies on aspects of participation, often undertaken by practitioner-researchers seeking to attune their services better to meet the aspirations of learners and potential learners. Properly, he locates the emergence of the work in a long-standing tradition of research into adult learning and social disadvantage. However, he identifies the important role Veronica played in introducing many to the work of Jacques Hédoux, one of a number of French social scientists investigating the everyday life of the working class. Hédoux's work looks at the link between active citizenship and adult learning. John Field argues that Hédoux's work is framed by the political context faced by the communities he studied. How far was Hédoux's analysis of the close linkage between active civic engagement and learning linked just to a militant male working class, whose ties were to a declining communist movement in a declining industrial area? John cites Veronica's work in reporting that men's social ties are characteristically weaker than women's, and as a result less likely to sustain active citizenship. He concludes that until the end of the 1990s as many questions as answers were raised on the nature and causality of the linkage.

Since then, as he reports, work on social capital has produced a more sophisticated account of the benefits and disbenefits of people's networks and ties. The work of the Wider Benefits of Learning Research Centre in particular has established that adult learning influences people's social connections. The evidence in the other direction is more conflicting. Some social relationships have a more positive impact on likelihood to engage with learning than others, as John Field's own work in Northern Ireland makes clear. Yet if the field is complex the research can nevertheless offer policy-makers signposts on the interventions most likely to enhance the life chances and empowerment of groups failed by initial education.

All in all, then, this is a collection of essays which celebrates the work of a distinguished scholar, maps the impact of widening access and participation studies and practices on public policy, and points to an acute failure of policy memory in post-school education and training. It is clear that, once again, the case needs to be made afresh that adults who have benefited least from earlier education need access to a rich mix of formal and informal learning oppor-tunities, they need flexible progression routes, and they need a system that respects what they bring to their studies. For adult learners the shortest route to a learning goal is seldom a straight line. However, the authors demon-strate, we know what works, given the resources and freedom to make it work. Winning the argument for those resources and freedoms remains as stiff a challenge today as it was two decades ago. Where from time to time advances have been made, imaginative vision has been accompanied by weaker, short-term policy gains. Yet as the authors also make clear, the struggle is far too important to give up. If we are to make ours a democracy where everyone's voice is valued, adult learning, life-long and life-wide, has a critical role to play.

References

DfES (1998) *The Learning Age*, London: DfES

Independent Committee of Inquiry into Student Finance (1999) *Student Finance: Fairness for the Future* (*The Cubie Report*), Edinburgh: Independent Committee of Inquiry into Student Finance

Kennedy, H. (1997) *Learning Works: Widening Participation in Further Education*, Coventry: FEFC

McGivney, V. (1990) *Education's for Other People: Access to Education for Non-Participant Adults*, Leicester: NIACE

McGivney, V. (1992) *Motivating Unemployed Adults to Undertake Education and Training: Some British and other European Findings*, Leicester: NIACE/REPLAN

McGivney, V. (1992) *The Women's Education Project in Northern Ireland*, Belfast: Women's Education Project

McGivney, V. (1993) *Women, Education and Training: Barriers to Access, Informal Starting Points and Progression Routes*, Leicester: NIACE

McGivney, V. (1994) *Wasted Potential: Training and Career Progression for Part-Time and Temporary Workers*, Leicester: NIACE

McGivney, V. (1999) *Excluded Men: Men who are Missing from Education and Training*, Leicester: NIACE

McGivney, V. (1999) *Informal Learning in the Community: A Trigger for Change and Development*, Leicester: NIACE

McGivney, V. (2000) *Recovering Outreach: Concepts, Issues and Practices*, Leicester: NIACE

McGivney, V. (2001) *Fixing or Changing the Pattern? Reflections on Widening Adult Participation in Learning*, Leicester: NIACE

National Committee on Inquiry into Higher Education (1997) *Higher Education in the Learning Society* (*The Dearing Report*), London: HMSO

Woodley, A., Wagner, L., Slowey, M., Hamilton, M., Fulton, O. (1987) *Choosing to Learn: Adults in Education*, Milton Keynes: SRHE/Open University Press

Chapter 2

Sides to middle – adult learning is for everyone

Ursula Howard

I want to start this chapter with three stories which I've heard recently from adult learners. Stories are at the heart of adult learning itself, and they are at least as important as numbers as evidence of its value to society. In any case, everyone wants stories and has stories of their own to tell, including government ministers. Stories are part of what makes us all human. I hope they will set a good context for this chapter, which is about the need to turn up the volume of the argument that everyone is a learner, that learning is for everyone, and about how we can discard the bad habits associated with the idea that we have to make 'hard choices' about who gets support and who does not.

The first story was told to me by a French-speaking taxi driver, Michel de H., in Brussels. He drove me to the airport after a long day's meeting I had attended to discuss the 'Lisbon goals': the eight key competences all citizens of the EU will need to survive and flourish in the twenty-first century. After a conversation about adult literacy, in which the driver showed great interest, he told me that his work was relevant to mine. He is not only a cab driver, but also a 'guide culturel' and an 'ecrivain publique'. All three roles are spelt out on his business card. He had had many jobs, but no formal qualifications. After many years he returned to education as a mature student to study social science and pedagogy. He now uses his education and skills in the community, not only as scribe, but also as the organiser of free public events which debate education, current affairs, peace and development. Taxi-driving is his long-term bread and butter income. He has a steady trickle of clients as a scribe, a service about which he expresses no surprise or concern. It is simply a function which every community needs, and he is committed to doing it. '*Il y a toujours des gens qui en a besoin*', he says, and he believes there always will be. The event flyer that Michel handed me talks of the education system in Belgium as in a state of crisis.

The second story is about a 31-year-old man in prison in England, serving a long sentence. It was told by a Quaker at a meeting in Oxford. The prisoner describes himself as having little education, low basic skills and no qualifications. He is struggling to read the National Geographic magazine and New Scientist, to help him study astronomy and ecology, which he has become passionate about and is determined to study. The members of the meeting were asked if they knew anyone with serious knowledge about either subject, who would be able to go into the prison on a voluntary basis and teach him, or rather informally guide his learning. Neither the subject matter, nor his preferred approach to learning were available as part of the prison education offer.

The third story is a partial *Skills for Life* success story. Again, this was a conversation in a taxi, this time in north London. As so often, the cab driver was interested in what I do for a living. I told her I work in educational research and that my work is about adults who have problems with reading, writing or maths or who are learning English. 'I'm one of those', she said straight back: 'I can't write'. She told me how well her teenage children were doing in school, passing exams, but that her spelling was 'absolutely dreadful'. She goes each week to a literacy class in Essex and works on spelling. She simply wants the skills, not as a route to anything else. She finds it hard, but the teacher makes it 'a fascinating subject'. She is determined to get the better of spelling, gets a kick out of making progress and tries not to miss sessions. She knows there is a test, and wants to be ready for it. It was her children's success at school which made her want to learn, although she'd always been 'terrible at every kind of writing'. Her only regret is that it is sometimes impossible to fit in her shift patterns and family activities with the set times of the classes. She thinks that her fluctuating attendance is holding her back. Prompted by a question from me, she thought it would be great if she could be given support from the college to fit extra study around the changing patterns of her life and work. There was not a trace of self-consciousness or anxiety about this lively conversation and we parted, warmly wishing each other good luck with our different work on literacy.

These stories offer a way in to some important questions about adult learning. All of them tell of the vibrancy and 'ordinariness' in Raymond Williams's sense, of adult learning and the ways in which it helps to weave individual lives into communities. They tell of people engaging in learning to suit their own ends, and as a 'social practice'. They also show that adult learning will not collapse if state funding collapses, but that some are crucially helped by strong state support. The stories also bring home the challenges which adult educators face in advocating adult learning in an era when policy priorities again and again put young people before older ones and economic aims before social concerns. The stories hint at critical questions of our time: who determines what is learned? What motivates people? In what circumstances does learning flourish? In what kinds of learning relationships? How can our system best support the practices of adult learners? Why do we face government snubs to adult learning with almost cyclical regularity, and especially to the well-established public and private value of learning for its own sake? Why do we often treat adults, who often know themselves what they want to learn, as if they were children about whose learning others know best? Is our (adult) education system in the UK also in a state of crisis?

NIACE is unique in Britain because it champions with equal vigour the learning needs of every adult who wants to learn, whatever their age, cultural background, income level or existing range of skills and knowledge. NIACE has never seen the need for either/ors in learning. Where there is inequality in access, they have spotted it, and NIACE campaigns have an integrity evidenced by the number of times they have swum fearlessly against the current of policy directions or challenged prevalent socio-educational thinking. Veronica McGivney was the first to explore why it is that men, for example, appeared to be disengaged from learning and how their needs could be better supported (McGivney, 1998). In any case, there is plenty of room and enough resources to champion the vastly disparate learning needs of those who have been least well served by their initial education, as well as those people with economic and educational success who want to go on learning throughout life. NIACE has always voiced the powerful economic as well as social and humanistic arguments to support the wisdom of an inclusive, continuing and well-supported adult learning infrastructure. NIACE has tirelessly gathered evidence from around the world, familiarising us with models from Scandinavia to Brazil to help us rethink adult learning in Britain and the relationship between state and society in sponsoring and supporting learning. In the late 1990s, the new Labour government set out a generous vision in policy documents such as *The Learning Age*, drawing on the strong informal learning traditions of this country (DfES, 1998). So why should there now be 'hard choices' to make in the fourth biggest economy in the world, with a government deeply conscious that knowledge and skills are critical to success, and with highly-educated nations committed to lifelong learning threatening fierce competition (DTI, 2000). On the other hand, why do adult educators express panic and gloom when one sponsor of adult learning, the state, reduces its financial support for formal adult learning, particularly the 'recreational' or 'liberal' kinds of learning? It doesn't add up.

What NIACE is up against, I will argue, is a deeper malaise, in educational theory and practice as well as policy. In policy, this malaise reveals itself as a mindset which insists that there are always 'hard choices to make'. It is not only a matter of limited funds, or even that in Britain we have become accustomed to a vast and still growing distance between the wealthy and the poor (Pearce, 2005). There is a reluctance to take tough enough measures to reduce wealth gaps, although income differentials have narrowed as a result of the anti-poverty policies of the last few years. Those with greater power and wealth are so well protected from undue burdens, including tax, that radical long-term change to support universal lifelong learning is always beyond reach. Short-term policy initiatives in adult learning, many of which are excellent and effective, are favoured. At the same time there is a continual restructuring of the national framework for planning, funding, inspecting, quality assuring and improving learning: forming, breaking up and reforming the jigsaw. These approaches have yet to prove that they create more success-ful, sustainable learning on the ground. They are symptomatic of an environment in which good policy intentions and clear strategic directions are implemented through disconnected, confusing and above all short-term actions. Social progress, a recent phrase in the aspirational discourse of post-16 educational policy, is unsurprisingly patchy and tentative.

Choice as a tool of policy is a double-edged concept. It is promoted in the interests of democracy, freedom, reducing inequality, ensuring the delivery of essential public services and giving people, for example parents in search of schools for their children, a say and a sense of active participation in what happens to them. But the language of choice also hints at, as well as obfuscates the fact that the state will not provide everything for everyone and thus normalises the competition for resources. Adult learning has been at the sharp end of that competition. Choice throws back the responsibility to people in society to ensure their own success, at the same time admonishing the less powerful with constant reminders that rights are the reward for responsibilities: they have to be earned.

I want to argue here that we need to develop a different mentality if we are to create an inclusive, learning society which also develops and redevelops skills to support a healthy economy. I will suggest ways in which we can take forward our own thinking, whether we are policy makers, educators, advocates, researchers or practitioners. Burrow under the concept of 'choice' and there is a starker mindset which prevents us from realising our vision. I will call this bi-polarity and I believe it runs deep and often unchallenged in our thinking and our values. What do I mean by bi-polarity? Dominant discourses are often characterised by binary opposites. Human beings tend to pit light against darkness and high (lofty) above low (squat); depth against shallowness, the sacred against the secular. There are good people and evil ones, a pure and simple split. In the past, responses to the physical world have also mirrored this view, offering metaphors for human values and cultural preferences. For example, it took most of the 19th century for people gradually to see the Grand Canyon as a place of awe-inspiring beauty, because aesthetic sensibilities were attuned to looking upwards for grandeur. The Alps were sublime; a massive hole in the ground was merely a scientific curiosity (Yeo, 1991; Pyne, 1999).

In education, the dominant opposites, laden with cultural values, include: intellectual and technical; vocational and academic; higher and elementary; arts and sciences; success and failure. In adult learning, common opposites include formal and informal; vocational and recreational; knowledge and skills; (social) inclusion and exclusion; young adults and older learners. More recently we also have 'supply' and 'demand', 'provider' and 'customer' in a marketised model, with educators at one end of the pole 'delivering' to learners at the other end, effectively splitting those who create, produce and offer from those who consume the choices presented to them.

In adult basic education, the oppositional debates focus firstly on what 'counts' or 'does not count' towards the government's PSA target, agreed with the Treasury in 2001. The target for the 10-year programme to address literacy and numeracy problems in England, *Skills for Life*, states that by 2010, 2.25 million people are to be helped to gain a whole, formally defined, qualification level in their literacy and numeracy skills. The levels are derived from a set of standards, which range from pre-entry at the bottom, through three 'sub-levels at 'entry' level, through level one and finally, to level two at the top of the reach of *Skills for Life*. Categorisation by level, bottom to top, is the cousin of polarisation. And once defined, categories must be capable of measurement. In *Skills for Life*, as in other policy areas, targets are set and met (or not) by the measurement of learners' achievements. However, measurement for inclusion in the target only starts at Entry level 3. This leads also to a polarised discourse of what does and does not count, and of 'target-bearing' and 'non-target bearing' provision. Despite the promotion of progress, progression and even qualifications below Entry level 3, what counts matters most. Thus, the target has created exclusion in a policy designed to support its opposite: inclusion. Learners likely to contribute relatively quickly to the target are more attractive to government departments, funding bodies and providers wishing, rightly, to continue to attract the support of the Treasury. What has happened is that the learners with the greatest needs, at the bottom of the level system, including those with learning difficulties, are less favoured than those in the middle, even though the policy was created precisely to help them. We have already stereotyped these groups of learners as 'hard to reach'. But we have made ourselves harder for them to reach: we are poles apart.

Bi-polar thinking is at the heart of this culture of classification, with its categorising of things and actions and its stereotyping of people within an often unconsciously applied set of assumed values. It has contributed to the highly developed state of division and exclusion, educational, social and economic in which we still live. Most importantly, bi-polarity neglects, or worse, ignores, the interdependency and constant interaction of so-called opposites and the dynamism between them – whether in individual human beings, or in society. In adult learning we cannot afford to bypass the complex realities and multiple levels of learners' lives, practices and achievements. Either/ors do not help us to support learners and learning. They diminish the range of possibilities which exist for supporting the variety of learning that people want and the meanings they wish to discover and pursue. As Jan Eldred has written: 'let us not fall into traps of generalisation or stereotyping . . . but let us offer a rich and wide range of learning opportunities which inspire, create awe and wonder, tap into motivations and purposes . . . That's the way to develop confidence, self-esteem and dignity . . . Entry level literacy learners are not entry level people.' (Eldred, 2006)

If we want to make Jan's vision happen, we need to find cures for our bi-polar disorders. For the millions of human beings who deal with this condition as part of their state of health and social being, whether as a mild or acute condition, the answer lies in multiple therapies, and combining some of the following: counselling and other talking cures; developing self-understanding and the ability to manage emotions; replacing bad drugs with good drugs, being physically active, getting enough sleep and adopting a healthy diet. What for? To be able to fold in the ends of the pole without breaking them off, to integrate them and occupy a more comfortable ground with a quieter self who lives nearer the middle of the range of feelings and possibilities. A person's goals might be to live and learn with yourself and others; to be sad without feeling depressed; to be content without living on a see-saw – soaring to heady heights, only to crash down again; to be creative without loss of control; to live with the interdependence of so-called opposites and the dynamism between them and to be able to integrate them; to be alone and individuated and to live in mutual dependence with and alongside others.

Using this metaphor, what could be gained for thinking differently and advocating action to overcome polarity and division in adult learning? Alan Tuckett's concept of 'seriously useless learning' challenges divisive approaches. In his 2005 inaugural professorial lecture at the University of Leicester, he analysed the history of adult learning in its wider political and social contexts, starting with the report of the 'Reconstruction Committee' set up in 1917. The 1919 report proposed an approach to adult learning to address the needs of an economically depressed, socially restless and deeply traumatised post-war world. It was a moment of ambition, recognising the complexity of needs and the critical importance of including everyone. The report recognised and celebrated the myriad forms of learning which had happened in civil society over the previous century, independent of state funding. They included in their definition of education:

> 'all the deliberate efforts by which men and women attempt to satisfy their thirst for knowledge, to equip themselves for their responsibilities as citizens and members of society, or to find opportunities for self-expression. (Waller, 1919)

However, the report goes on to argue that this great tradition of learning, so much of it within working class communities, is different from: 'formal organised education which is carried on by means of classes and systematic study'. The learning of 'mutual improvement societies…naturalists' societies and the creative work of the craftsman' are seen as separate from classes. Nevertheless, as well as the beginnings of the split we still live with, this report represented a moment in which the vision and possibility of an integrated approach to adult learning was alive. The report sought to promote the use of voluntary and mutual organisations, trade unions and adult schools as the basis from which to grow a more systematic adult education provision with more state funding. The committee itself, as Tuckett points out, also worried about the impact of state funding on the vibrancy of civil society organisations and the controls which the state might want over curriculum and participation in return for its money. But the idea was to have both: to support one through the other. This was also the period with the richest fabric of 'social capital' to weave adult learning into. Yet state funding soon ended up on a trajectory where it, and its professional agents, funded what they thought best. Despite the close and enduring links with the Scandinavian culture of adult learning, with its much more permissive and permeable boundaries between the state and local communities, 'adult education' and informal, mutual learning gradually grew apart.

The history of this split goes back further. Throughout the 19th century, before the advent of universal state education, mutual improvement societies, the voluntarily-founded Mechanics Institutes, radical and reforming groups who pursued 'really useful knowledge', and the web of 'private' working-class schools in local communities formed powerful networks and cultures of self-determined learning at very local levels. (Rose, 2001; Gardner, 1984). This was recognised and celebrated by David Blunkett in his well-known introduction to the 1998 Green Paper, *The Learning Age*. However, in the drive towards universal elementary education these forms were discouraged, attacked, patronised or taken over by the middle class, in the contest for control over learning. Some organisations and practices collapsed, others survived through transformation and rebirth into organisations like the WEA. As the state took a grip, an opportunity was missed to integrate existing forms and practices which had emerged from communities and educational movements with the state's legitimate interest in channelling skills and knowledge for the wider economic and social good. Formal and informal learning were separated: top-down systems were put in place at national and local authority levels and informal learning declined as part of diminishing levels of 'social capital'. Civil society was weakened in relation to the state. The gain was an education system, with entitlement alongside compulsion. But the losses were felt for decades, as testified by many commentators from communities. And many parents were bewildered by the new and inflexible curricula and pass/fail culture imposed on their children (Vincent, 2003).

Real, material divisions and polarities do actually exist. It would be naive to ignore them. This chapter cannot sufficiently explore the extent to which they result from bi-polar thinking or lead to it. Adults with literacy or numeracy needs, or refugee or immigrant families who live in the UK without spoken English adequate for their needs at work or daily life are at one end of the pole, socially and economically. Hedge-fund managers, policy makers and university professors are at the other. This illustrates the persistence of one very old system of classifying people. That system is the classification of people according to whether they do mental or manual work for a living, then creating and perpetuating social class and cultural divisions based on their occupations.

A large-scale national survey, conducted by the DfES to inform the *Skills for Life* strategy in England, which is planned to run from 2001 to 2010, clearly sets out the persistence of these divisions, and their impact: 'adults living in households in social class I were roughly four times as likely as those in social class V to reach Level 2 or above in the literacy test ... A similar difference in performance was noted in the numeracy test' (DfES, 2003). This survey uses a now standard classification system for sorting people into a social hierarchy. In addition, the survey testing regime (known as adaptive testing) was designed to measure the highest skills of a person, defined by where they first stumbled over a question. At that point, they were referred back to easier items. Thus the survey turns a person with low skills in one domain into a low-skilled person. Surveys such as this do not show what else a person might be able to do, for example answering a different, harder question, or demonstrating knowledge of astronomy. The survey follows a vertical system of levels to describe literacy and numeracy skills, or the lack of them. It also brings home a stark truth, if not explicitly named: that there is gross inequality in an education system which enables middle-class professional families to pass on success to their children, and disables families in which employment is manual or low-skilled and poorly paid.

To stay with literacy and numeracy, *Skills for Life* was explicitly intended to lessen this class-based polarity, focusing on those burdened with the greatest depth of disadvantage from their initial education experiences; or the most vulnerable ESOL learners, refugees, immigrants and asylum seekers, many of whom are not literate in their own different languages and coping with a different alphabet. At its outset, *Skills for Life* was intended as a 'crusade' to enable learners to improve their skills and capabilities; to help them to move up the levels by the creation and application of an ambitious infrastructure for learning, with standards, curricula, levels of achievement, assessments and tests. To meet the needs of all, starting with the most low skilled, the *Skills for Life* learning infrastructure starts at pre-entry level, and includes three sub-levels at 'entry level', suggesting a sophisticated recognition of the fine-tuned, layered curriculum and the ambitious scale of provision necessary to reach the most disadvantaged. But the implementation of policy has not yet entirely followed its initial aims and values. These were articulated clearly in the report of the Moser working party, set up by the Government in 1998 as a result of the international OECD survey (IALS) which had revealed the extent of the UK's problems. These aims were to address social exclusion, inequality and the economic disbenefits of low skills by a strategy to tackle the problems of the lowest skilled adults. However, the curriculum and assessment models were too rapidly drawn up and overly derivative of the schools strategies to fully meet the needs of adults. They are neither flexible nor sensitive enough to the needs of adult learners with the greatest learning needs and are ripe for review. There has been too little time to fully professionalise the teaching profession to meet such a high-speed implementation of policy and the quality of teaching and learning remains a big challenge. But the major policy driver, as I have argued above, was the ambitious PSA target which, once set, has to be met. It was defined in a way that enabled 16–18-year-old full-time learners to be counted and to capture the achievements of learners who were taking already-existing, related qualifications at levels 1 and 2, such as key skills or GCSEs. The consequence has been that a very large number of people with skills just below the threshold for the target (Entry level 3), have achieved level 1, and many thousands have moved from level 1 to level 2. ESOL learners have also boosted numbers, especially in large conurbations. All these groups eased the route to a successful interim achievement of the target in 2004. This does not mean that learners at pre-entry and entry levels have been ignored. It is to the credit of *Skills for Life* that many thousands more adult learners and ESOL learners than ever before have been funded to learn. It is just that the core target group has, oddly, become increasingly problematic for the strategy and the subject of uneasiness and controversy, rather than unequivocally holding the status of top priority. That is, adults with skills at pre-entry and entry level. We are forced to ask how important the learners with the lowest skills really are to a strategy which was designed precisely for them. It appears that adults, now that funding is tighter, are a problem, especially if they need a long time, as many do, to progress through the entry levels, or are not mentally or psychologically ready to take approved qualifications – if indeed they, or their employers, need or want them.

Research has shown what a huge effect very low skills can have on people's lives and the multiple benefits to them of participating in learning. A recent study for the National Research and Development Centre for Adult Literacy and Numeracy (NRDC) by John Bynner and Samantha Parsons (2006) examined the literacy and numeracy skills and practices of 10,000 people born in 1970 through interviews and formal assessments. Their children were also included in the study. Bynner and Parsons have shown that people whose skills are at 'Entry level 2' and below in the English system of levels are clearly and significantly more adversely affected by their literacy skills than people at just one level higher – Entry level 3. Their problems with reading, writing and maths are associated with greater mental and physical health problems, poor job prospects, poverty, loneliness and isolation. Participation in civic life and political processes is lower. What is more, there are intergenerational cycles of disadvantage: the young children of adults with skills at Entry level 2 and below are more likely to struggle with pre-school and primary school learning. Few people want to acknowledge their learning needs, even if the assessments show an objective problem. They often have good reasons for that. However, those people who do acknowledge their learning needs also reap more benefits. The improvement to their literacy and numeracy can change their lives to a greater extent than those who have already achieved more skills. That will also contribute to economic and social well-being – provided the investment in their learning is made (Bynner and Parsons, 2006). That investment would include, realistically, providing several hundred hours for each level of attainment and offering innovative, flexible support for adult learners to help with self-study periods when, like all adults with responsibilities in life, they cannot attend (Comings, 1999; Porter *et al*, 2005). Adult literacy is a long-term problem. It is served by a medium-term strategy, which is in danger of going for short-term gains which will not remove the fundamental problem. If this should happen, the polarised state of learning and skills would remain in place and the opportunity to lessen it would have been wasted.

Consistent with its economic, rather than social, focus, the *Skills for Life* strategy aims to raise the skills of individual learners, especially young people and those in work, with an assessment (measurement) regime explicitly geared to include young people and the school-based assessments which they routinely undertake. Parents are also targeted, and family learning is both popular and successful. Children's learning is a great motivator of adult learning. But the needs of older adults and anyone over 65 are invisible. Over 65s are excluded from most national surveys for example, despite the rapidly changing demographies of the workplace. People will work longer and get smaller pensions. Age discrimination legislation underlines the reality of the need to keep older people in the workforce. All of this means learning and relearning, continuously or episodically, formally and informally, throughout life. That goes for everyone, not only people with low skills. Policy also remains impervious to the importance of so-called 'soft skills', as opposed to 'hard' ones: the affective learning gains such as self-confidence, engaging with other people positively, listening and speaking appropriately and learning from others, all of which employers value, and do not see as 'soft', but which are harder to measure. Badly needed as they are, they count for little.

What can educators do to create a more holistic way of thinking in the interests of adult learners? Literacy theory offers one alternative to an overly skills-based model: the social practice approach. This stresses the nature of literacy as about communication, in society, family and community. And the benefits of learning as about the ability to practice literacy and numeracy as an individual in a wide variety of contexts. Policy makers have not been able to recognise the potential of such models to support employment and enterprise.

Responsibility for the narrowness, or polarisation of approaches lies with educators as well as policy makers. Bi-polar thinking exists in the academy as well. Apart from new research for the NRDC at Lancaster University (Ivanic and Tseng, 2005; Barton *et al*, 2006), the practical power and practical applications of the social practice approach and its relationship to skills, has not been strongly advocated. Instead, social practice is pitted against the impoverished skills model, which is typecast as addressing only adults' deficits in skills, and by implication, as people. The learning of skills could be conceptualised by 'social practice' thinkers as the pre-requisite for and an essential element of any practice of literacy and numeracy. If the two discourses and models could meet each other in the middle, a more integrated, conceptual framework could be developed which recognises the skills in social practice and the social practice in skills. This would have the potential to be much more powerful, and empowering, to learners than either, as they now stand, polarised. The skills model is isolated and demonised; the social practice model has no influence on policy. Skills which are divorced from context, assumed absent, mechanically learned, tested as a tick-box, multiple choice exercise will not be adequate to the changing demands of work or family or leisure. Neither does such an approach develop properly the thinking skills or creativity of learners in ways which will enable them to make sustainable progress. Research has shown that learning maths by thinking through problems with others, for example, is attractive and effective, compared to traditional pedagogies which seek the 'right answer' (or focus on the 'wrong' answer). These discourage many adult learners and children. Learning to write for self-expression builds a learner's sense that they have something to say – and can say it at work on email or in a personal letter. Using language as well as consuming it is critical to building a higher skilled economy and an active citizen. If *Skills for Life* does not grasp this nettle, its limitations will be exposed, sooner rather than later. Equally, social practice models need to be translated and developed for teacher educators and teachers into clear practical applications, so that they become part of classroom practice. The proponents of the two approaches need to get together. A dialogue is badly needed and NIACE would be well placed to broker it.

Government spokespeople routinely offer assurances that economic and social inclusion are convergent: that getting a job is the basis of social inclusion. Such a framework is reassuring, but still leaves a lot of people out. Yet adult learning policies are clearly based on the belief that they are helping to reduce inequality and cycles of deprivation. Despite the dominance of the economic, there are successful programmes which focus on the social and social partnership approaches to adult lives in and beyond work: The Adult Community Learning Fund and the Trade Union Learning Fund and Family Learning expose the contradictions in a policy which cannot escape from the tight grip of economic drivers, yet tries to address wider problems. An uneasy settlement is the result, in which a utilitarian, economic model dominates. Social inclusion, often characterised as 'reaching the hard-to-reach' remains elusive. Research suggests that if a practically-applied social approach were to dominate, the economic domain might actually gain more than at present (Barton *et al*, 2006). A more mutually motivating cooperation between policy and practice could fertilise some common ground on which policy and practice could, working together, promise richer, more successful learning to support individual, social an economic benefits.

At the other end of our adult learning pole are the keen, often educationally qualified, people wanting to learn for learning's sake. Funding to support their learning is threatened repeatedly and the outlook for the coming years is bleak. Highly qualified adults have many reasons to go on learning, and cannot necessarily afford it among their complex commitments. Yet research from NIACE, for example on learning and health, and the work of the Wider Benefits of Learning Research Centre has convincingly shown the economic and social case of investing in adults across the social spectrum and at all ages. People who learn live longer, healthier lives; they contribute better to the economy; they are more likely to be active, tolerant citizens; they pass on learning habits to their children and are more likely to participate in civic and political life.

If resources are scarce, let us think creatively about how to use them differently, including to support learning that is already happening, formally and informally. Perhaps adult educators need to control less and facilitate more. Research for the Learning and Skills Development Agency (LSDA) showed the fluidity and creative overlap which exists in practice between formal and informal adult learning and the increasing mix of private and publicly generated learning activity (Colley, Hodkinson and Malcolm, 2003). Participation in funded adult learning still reflects a divide between the educational haves and have-nots. So we put much effort into defending adult learning which attracts those who have already benefited from the system. We know it is hard for adults to learn continuously, in regular two-hour slots. Research in the USA by Steve Reder has shown adults' willingness to engage in supported self-study, whether they are graduates or learners struggling to read and write. Yet our system still persists with its institutions and timetables, in an age where ICT affords very different approaches, and we know the value of mentors, coaches, brokers and sponsors of learning. Could we put more effort into supporting individual and collective self-study as core to more flexible, responsive, locally-based teaching and learning? (Reder, 2005)

And a lot of other learning is happening, quite outside the 'system'. If we put more energy into finding out about, thinking about and nurturing informal learning, helping it to gain recognition and respect as knowledge, we could develop a less polarised learning world. The list of learning activities and activities involving learning in local communities, and increasingly online is endless and happens without state support, from establishing credit unions, to gyms, to horticultural societies to local branches of Amnesty. As yet, apart from NIACE's initiatives, we have not created a strong sense of these as a central part of adult learning. The traditional adult education classes, for example those of the WEA and LCC, incorporated them in their provision, at least in the early decades of the twentieth century. Courses led by the Chrysanthemum Society, on keeping pigeons, or care of the horse, as well as informal but purposeful social events were part of the adult learning of that era when the boundaries between adult education and community activity were fuzzier. We need a theoretical grasp of what they could mean now – beyond the concept of social capital – as legitimate and essential learning of knowledge and skills. Stephen Jay Gould wrote about this as the need to bridge the gap between science and the wider culture. Millions of people, he argued, love and practise science, 'learning the feel of true expertise in a chosen expression'. He cites the sophisticated knowledge of underwater ecology among tropical fish enthusiasts, in the USA mainly working-class men; the horticultural knowledge of millions of mainly older middle-class women; the astronomical learning of telescope enthusiasts; and most obviously to millions of parents, 'the mental might', including in the classification and correct spelling, of 'hideously complex dinosaur names' among five-year-olds (Gould, 2000). The incidence of expertise, and active learning, is likely to be spread across social classes and 'skill levels'. We should find ways of confirming and celebrating this in irrefutable evidence. John Field, in his book *Lifelong Learning and the New Order* argued that we already live in a learning culture. But it remains exclusive, especially to those with learning difficulties and other disempowered groups (Field, 2000). What Gould's analysis offers is the point that if millions of people of all ages, cultures and classes recognised the status of their activity and knowledge as science, 'democracy would shake hands with the academy' and then the state, enabled by the adult learning community, could 'harvest' their fascination with knowledge in the service of more general education'. In Mexico, the project 'los saberes de la vida' conducted a survey of 50,000 people in different communities to find out what they already know and can do – and what they want to learn next – as the basis of state support for learning. We could aim for no less than the democratisation of knowledge, recognising and respecting what people know and helping them to learn what they want to learn, in a rich and interactive mix of independent and state supported learning. That way we can help strengthen civil society, supporting learning which is organic to people's needs and desires. We can celebrate what is already happening as much as decrying what is not. We can see knowledge as something to be shared and passed on, often in mutual ways, and not only in mutal organisations. That is the promise of the prison story (Yeo, 2000). And, by reducing false polarities and divisions, adult educators can do even more to help to strengthen our ailing democracy.

The image in my mind as I end this piece is a common domestic practice in the age of post-second-world-war frugality. When a bed sheet was worn out in the middle, it was cut up and skilfully resewn, with the fresh, hidden and unworn sides brought to the middle, giving a valuable and essential item a new lease of useful life. The different parts of the whole were thus used in different ways, at different times. This is relevant again, in the post-waste era of sustainability. In adult learning, everyone should be seen, valued and their skills and attributes recognised and - in the most positive sense of the word – used for the benefit of everyone.

References

Barton *et al* (2006) *Relating Adults' Lives and Learning: Participation and Engagement in Different Settings*, London: NRDC

Bynner, J. and Parsons, S. (2006) *New Light on Literacy and Numeracy*, London: NRDC

Colley, H., Hodkinson, P. and Malcolm, J. (2003) *Informality and Formality in Learning*, London: LSDA

Comings, J. (1999) *Persistence Among Adult Basic Education Students in Pre-GED Classes*, NCSALL

DfES (1998) *The Learning Age*, London: DfES

DfES (2003) *The Skills for Life Survey: A National Needs and Impact Survey of Literacy, Numeracy and ICT Skills*, London: DfES

DTI (2000) *Our Competitive Future: Building the Knowledge-Driven Economy*, London: DTI

Eldred, J. (2006) 'The entry level debate', *Reflect* 5, April 2006

Field, J. (2000) *Lifelong Learning and the New Order*, Stoke-on-Trent: Trentham

Gardner, P. (1984) *The Lost Elementary Schools of Victorian England*, London: Croon Helm

Gould S. J. (2000) *The Lying Stones of Marrakech*, Jonathan Cape

Ivanic, R. and Tseng, M. (2005) *Understanding the Relationships Between Learning and Teaching: An Analysis of the Contribution of Applied Linguistics*, London: NRDC

McGivney, V. (1998) *Excluded Men: Men who are Missing from Education and Training*, Leicester: NIACE

Pearce, N. (2005) *Basic Skills and Social Principles: An Anglo-Social Model, NRDC lecture series*. Available at www.nrdc.org.uk

Porter, K., Cuben, S., Comings, J. with Chase, V. (2005) *One Day I Will Make It: A Story of Adult Student Persistence*, London: NRDC

Pyne, S. (1999) *How the Canyon Became Grand: A Short History*, USA: Penguin Putnam Inc.

Reder, S. (2005) *Literacy and the Lifecourse*, Reflect 1, 2005

Rose, J. (2001) *The Intellectual Life of the British Working Classes*, New Haven and London: Yale University Press

Vincent, D. M. (2003) 'The progress of literacy', *Victorian Studies*, Spring 2003

Waller, R. (1919) *A Design for Democracy*, London: Max Parrish

Yeo, S. (1991) 'Access: What, whither, when and how?', Mansbridge Memorial Lecture, University of Leeds, pp. 1–36

Yeo, S. (1996) 'Work and learning, learning and work: on changing the conversation', *Studies in the Education of Adults*, 28(1): 1–13

Yeo, S. (2000) *Organic Learning: Mutual Enterprise and the Learning and Skills Agenda*, Leicester: NIACE

Chapter 3

Time to use the F word again

Jane Thompson

We don't hear very much about discrimination against women anymore. Much less, women's oppression or women's rights. To have such concerns requires feminist consciousness. But feminism is now the sort of world-view which, like socialism, Marxism and even liberalism, is *so* last century. It embodies ideas and ways of understanding social relationships that New Labour in the UK, and the neo-cons in the US, have both derided and denounced in pursuit of less critical and more mordernising ideologies. These days it is individualism, consumerism, pragmatism and managerialism that serve to legitimise, rather than to challenge, the real hegemony of capitalist patriarchy. At least in the rich countries of the Global North.

Although we might think that Western enlightenment, the suffragettes and women's liberation all helped to invent and re-invent feminism, ours is an intellectual and political tradition that also repeatedly consigns questions of sexual inequality and repression to the dustbin of history. If you go looking for the energy and idealism that characterise feminist ways of knowing, which have meaning and relevance to women's lives today, you will find them in the words and deeds of women anti-poverty, health and education activists across the Global South. But you will be lucky to find similar analysis and conviction made manifest in equivalent civil society organisations and public bodies in Blair's Britain.

Why is this? Maybe the battle is won. Could it be that the kinds of restrictions that were imposed on women in the past by economic and political inequalities, religious and cultural ideas, biological and psychological beliefs, no longer apply? Maybe second-wave feminism played a part in changing perceptions and aspirations. The liberal predominance of moderate and increasingly corporate versions of feminism, at the expense of more radical and uncompromising positions, no doubt melded more easily into the mainstream. More jobs for the girls in institutions controlled by the boys can be viewed as a victory of sorts. Some, at least, of the emerging trends serve to plot what looks like progress. Especially in relation to education and employment.

Equality for some

Back in the seventies and eighties feminist writers revealed an education system in which young women were 'learning to lose' (Spender, 1982) and a labour market in which it was widely assumed that women worked only for pin money (Coote and Campbell, 1982; Westwood, 1984). Those who joined the Second Chance for Women programme in Southampton, for example, did so in a climate whereby women wanting qualifications and decent jobs were given a very hard time by the men in their lives and by the educational institutions they aspired to (Thompson, 1983; Thompson with the Taking Liberties Collective, 1989). But twenty years on we find that girls are 13 per cent more likely than boys to get 5+ A to C grades at GCSE and 9 per cent more likely to get 2+ A levels. In 2005 women are in the majority (by 20 per cent) when it comes to LSC funded provision in further education colleges and outnumber men in all subject areas, except for technical and manu-facturing, engineering and construction. The same pattern is true of higher education – except in relation to physical sciences, computer science, engineering and technology. Fifty-seven per cent of all HE qualifications are now awarded to women. In addition, women comprise 77 per cent of learners in adult and community learning and predominate in all forms of post-compulsory education except for work-based learning (McGivney, 2005). The participation and achievement of women from all ethnic backgrounds is such that any concern about gender is usually expressed in terms of excluded men.

In similar vein, women no longer say, 'I don't work, I'm only a housewife'. Sixty-seven per cent of women aged 16-64 go out to work, 56 per cent of them part-time. In the world's fifth richest economy, in which divorce rates are the highest in Europe, work is a necessity, as much as a source of financial independence for women. Women are increasingly the sole bread-winners in single parent families and co-breadwinners in families that routinely require two incomes to support the high cost of living in contemporary Britain. At the more lucrative end of the earnings scale, women appear more visible in business and as lawyers, doctors, politicians, media journalists and TV presenters than they were in the 1980s. Popular wisdom now presumes that free choice, good qualifications and hard work are what count when it comes to promotion, rather than institutional demarcations based on sex and gender.

But the same trends also serve to disguise some enduring problems as well as ignore some persisting inequalities. Although women are increasingly out-classing men in education, they still have a long way to go when it comes to parity of esteem and career power in the workplace. The subject choices of men and women remain significantly gendered and are connected to job opportunities that reflect a segregated labour market. Take Modern Appren-ticeships, for example. Young women are usually to be found in childcare, clerical training, hairdressing, health and social care – much as they ever were – whilst young men opt for plumbing, construction, the motor trade and electro-technical trades. Without the benefit of feminist analysis this might seem to be the consequence of choice, except that in education and guidance, as we know, supply most usually acts to inform demand. And personal advisers from Connexions rarely point out the obvious advantages of earning three or four times more as a plumber than by becoming a hairdresser. Of course, young people's gender identities are well learned by the time they leave school, including their assumptions about what are appropriate jobs for women and men.

Maturity seems to make little difference. An analysis of the calls made to Learndirect throughout 2004 revealed that men most often wanted to know about financial rewards, whereas women cited job satisfaction and doing something socially worthwhile as their main motivation for vocational training. Whilst the latter might represent public spirited and responsible qualities – which ought to be attractive to modern employers, who are said to require workers with team spirit and good people skills – it doesn't prevent them paying full-time women workers an hourly rate that is 18 per cent less on average than men's. Even when they are doing the same jobs. Women graduates, after five years in employment, earn 15 per cent less than men who have the same qualifications. And when it comes to average weekly incomes, the gender gap between men's and women's incomes in the UK is one of the highest in Europe, at 46 per cent (ONS, 2004; Women and Equality Unit, 2004). And all this thirty years after the Equal Pay Act became law in 1975.

The situation for part-time workers is even worse, more than three-quarters of whom are women. In a recent investigation by the Equal Opportunities

Commission (2005), it is revealed that 5.6 million of Britain's 7 million part-time workers have the skills and aspirations to perform well in higher-level jobs. Part-time women workers earn 40 per cent less per hour than men working full-time – which is much the same as thirty years ago – and are being sidelined into low-grade jobs that do not allow them to use their skills or fulfil their earnings potential. The Equal Opportunities Commission blames old-fashioned thinking in the boardroom and trade unions for what is still an unacceptable polarisation in the workplace. Whilst British men are working amongst the longest hours in the European Union, leading to an epidemic of job-related stress, women part-timers are being consigned to low-paid jobs with no prospects. They mostly work as shop assistants, care assistants or cleaners. Only 4 per cent are managers or senior officials.

What employers call flexibility, trade unions call exploitation. The spectacle of low-paid, middle-aged Asian women, being sacked by megaphone by Gate Gourmet during the summer of 2005, in order to hire cheaper agency workers, mainly from Somalia and Eastern Europe, is emblematic of a labour market in which poverty wages are endemic and the poorest help to enrich the rest of us by making domestic work, the food industry, catering and other luxury services cost less. It's a situation that politicians show no interest in addressing. Like Thatcherism in the 1980s, New Labour also believes in the autonomy of the free market. The government's only interference, the minimum wage, is still less than £6 an hour after eight years of unprecedented economic growth. Whilst the CBI warns of economic ruin whenever the rate rises, minimum wage jobs are growing, not shrinking (Toynbee, 2005).

So we have a labour market that continues to thrive on sex inequality – both in terms of occupational segregation and wage rates. And a political system that rarely considers this an issue. Housework and childcare remain the main responsibility of women, especially in poorer families, which is why women are still considered to be less reliable workers as well as being blamed for poor parenting skills when they happen to live in run-down neighbourhoods. Poverty and low wages have a knock-on effect on pensions. Women live longer than men but are much poorer in old age. Only 56 per cent of women workers are members of occupational, personal or stakeholder pension schemes, and of those aged 25 to 59 in 2001/02, a mere quarter had made pension contributions in each of the preceding ten years (Department of Work and Pensions, 2004; Pension Policy Institute, 2003). As a consequence, women can expect to live on incomes that are 44 per cent lower than men's by the time they are 65 and older.

Mars or Venus

In these circumstances, the unexamined sexism of the past – which led the man-in-the-street and the men with power to explain social and economic inequalities as biological and psychological inevitabilities – is probably less blatant than it once was, but we should not underestimate the attraction of natural explanations for ideological and political phenomena. The popular perception that men and women are so different they practically live on different psychological planets is still a fashionable ideology (Gray, 1992). How else can we explain little girls obsessed with pop stars and painting their nails, whilst little boys take over the playground with football and war games? At the same time, less attention is given to the studies that show when a country fosters women's financial independence, women are less likely to be attracted by rich men. Or that whilst women in Americanised countries like Britain are twice as likely as men to suffer depression, the difference disappears in much more gender-equal Scandinavia (James, 2005).

Insights such as these are addressed in a recent important study emerging from the University of Wisconsin-Madison, that weighs a vast amount of research evidence, examining everything from verbal reasoning and spatial perception, to aggression and frequency of smiling. The study concludes that in 78 per cent of respects, the psychological differences between men and women are either non-existent or insignificant. The findings are important because they do not present women and men as alike in every way but as being very much more similar than they are different. This matters when it comes to the personal costs of inflated claims made about difference in the workplace, at home and in relationships.

The widespread belief that women 'naturally' focus on caring while men 'naturally' focus on achievement, for example, only serves to reinforce the stereotype that fathers are less good at nurturing children, whilst women who violate the feminine ideal of being nurturing and nice can be penalised in both the workplace and wider society. Women in positions of leadership and political responsibility, when they are portrayed as uncaring autocrats, are viewed much more critically than men would be. The same goes for young women who engage in antisocial behaviour or criminal activities. Because they all display traits that seem to run counter to 'natural' behaviour. Taken overall the study provides one of the strongest ever scientific foundations for equal-sex social policies arguing that, in terms of gender difference, men and women start as blank slates (Hyde, 2005).

Learning for work

More men (79 per cent) than women (67 per cent) are employed in the labour market. Those who are registered as unemployed are about the same. Women significantly outnumber men in all forms of post compulsory and adult education except with respect to work-based learning. But because men are in the majority in work-based initiatives – such as Employer Training Pilots, Skills Sector Pilots and projects supported by the Union Learning Fund, as well as Modern Apprenticeships, New Deal for Young People and New Deal for the Long-Term Unemployed – the overall participation rates of men and women in learning are about the same. Although women are entering the labour market in increasing numbers, training for the workplace has a decidedly masculine focus compared to adult and community learning, and family learning, for example.

It is now well known that New Labour's flirtation with lifelong learning – defined in broad and generous ways in the early days – has been short-lived. *The Learning Age* (DfES, 1998), the establishment of the Learning and Skills Council, *21st Century Skills* (DfES, 2003) and now *Agenda for Change* (LSC, 2005) reflect an increasingly employer-centred and employment focus to what counts as lifelong learning. Although the Blunkett vision of a learning society in 1998 was about much more than work, the government has consistently and systematically prioritised employability, making it absolutely clear in 2003, that it would 'strengthen the supply of skills to deliver what employers want in they way they want it' (DfES, 2003). When subjected to closer inspection, 'much of the policy interest in lifelong learning is in fact preoccupied with the development of a more productive and efficient workforce' (Field, 2000).

It's a focus that – even in its own terms – is extremely unlikely to be successful because of the free market structure of the labour market. There are too many jobs, too many regions and too many sectors where the demand for skills is not sufficient to absorb an increased supply of skilled workers with aspirations heightened by education. As we have seen, the segregated, feminised and racialised nature of the labour market is such that women, migrant workers and minority ethnic workers function well below their potential, so that employers can continue to make profits on low-priced, standardised goods and services, in the interests of a 'strong economy'. It isn't in the employers' interests to give low paid workers an inflated sense of their own worth or capabilities by making more education easily available. And a skills strategy that suggests otherwise is either extremely naive or deliberately misleading. Although improved access to education is vital in a complex and changing world, education alone cannot increase women's prosperity unless they also have access to high-quality jobs, equal pay, decent housing and good health.

Widening participation in higher education, to encourage more and different young women to secure degrees, does not guarantee them jobs commensurate with their qualifications, or create a labour market in which academic achievement and qualifications are necessarily well rewarded financially. The New Labour assumption that learning is undertaken to achieve material rewards and that learning automatically leads to jobs is not borne out by the evidence (Rees, Fevre and Furlong, 1997). According to Bowman and her colleagues, many people simply do not accept the link between educational achievement and work opportunities. They know from experience that, despite their qualifications, the work opportunities available to them are often restricted, their qualifications are not always valued and employers often appoint people for reasons other than their qualifications. For many, the consequences of participating in education are significantly different 'from those claimed by policy makers, education providers and benefit advisers' who are seen to be seriously out of step with people's lived realities (Bowman, Colley and Hodkinson, 2004).

In addition, the focus on younger adults in higher education policy-making and provision, with its attendant fee structure and debt implications, is a deterrent to older learners from ordinary backgrounds who might have expected lifelong learning to open up opportunities rather than close them down.

For those who are now called priority learners – those who can be employed, those with low levels of literacy, language and numeracy skills, those whose behaviour gives cause for concern – learning is becoming less and less a matter of choice. For growing numbers of people, particularly those who are in paid employment (because of regulatory frameworks, statutory requirements, contract compliance and customer or client expectations), or who are unemployed (because of Benefit and New Deal requirements), or who are seeking British citizenship (because of naturalisation requirements), or who are the subject of parenting orders (related to truanting and anti-social behaviour orders) much of what is described as adult learning is no longer voluntary but has become obligatory (Field, 2001).

The main problems with policies such as these can be summarised as follows:

- They are preoccupied with 'learning for earning' at the expense of informal or curiosity-driven learning and emancipatory learning.
- Authority and influence has been given over to business interests and employers in preference to educational experts and learners themselves.
- They concentrate on the supply side of provision whilst claiming to be responsive to demand.
- They continue to blame individuals and providers for problems which are structural or systemic in nature.
- They reflect a managerialist culture of control from the centre, underpinned by rigid systems of bureaucracy and accountability.

Learning for life?

Writing in 1983 I showed that women were both visible and invisible in adult education (Thompson, 1983). Twenty years on, women are still the majority of learners and front-line practitioners in a service that is largely shaped, managed and led by men in the most senior positions. Women learners outnumber men by roughly three to one in local authority provision, the WEA, Skills for Life, family learning and distance learning (McGivney, 2004). You only have to step inside the average classroom, or attend any practitioner training event, to see that adult and community learning is women's terrain. But although women have consistently supported adult learning activities, sometimes in large numbers, the practices and ideologies that combine to make the service what it is have not usually made women's involvement a matter of significance or the cause for celebration.

Adult learning has been slow to respond to the real interests of its participants and has served to reinforce traditional assumptions that militate against women's progress towards equality. Until the 1980s the curriculum took for granted women's domestic and dependent roles within the family and acted to support and reinforce them (McGivney, 2004). The influence of feminists did a great deal to challenge both the values and the focus of provision for a while, at a time when radical adult education was the ally of progressive social movements such as feminism, the peace movement, the trade union movement and the anti-racist movement. For many women, the experience of feminist adult education was the catalyst that was to change their circumstances and their lives forever (Thompson with the Taking Liberties Collective, 1989).

Twenty years on, in a very different political climate, the learning that is consumed by women is now re-invented once again, according to the language of self-improvement, confidence building, life skills and self-esteem. It supports the familiar remedial model that was once the anathema of feminist adult educators, rich in negative stereotypes about teenage mothers, Asian women, single parents and the unhealthy inhabitants of run-down neighbourhoods, all deemed to be 'at risk' of social exclusion. All of them prime targets for any number of small-scale projects, short-term initiatives, and grand government strategies, designed to micro-manage and improve the lifestyles of the lower orders.

The literature of funding applications, project reports and evaluation exercises is full of claims by policy makers and practitioners alike that interventions targeted at so-called non traditional learners and socially excluded groups – the majority of whom turn out to be women – give rise to increased confidence and self esteem (Eldred *et al*, 2005). I had thought that this was an essentially Western phenomenon until I read recently in Sierra Leone – a small West African country emerging from eleven years of civil war with a ranking of last in the world in the Human Development Index – that 'the experience of social exclusion from decision-making bodies and processes, the lack of educational opportunities, early marriage and the demands of childbearing and rearing causes many women to *suffer from low self-esteem and a lack of confidence* in their judgement' (Von Kotze, 2005, my emphasis). This must surely be the language of the writer rather than the assessment of the women in question but indicates just how pervasive – even in the context of extreme poverty and genocide – this current preoccupation has become.

It is easy to see why practitioners are attracted to policies that seem to focus on women's personal and emotional development in an apparently supportive and benign way, despite the fact that there is little agreement about what self esteem actually is, and virtually no convincing evidence about its effects or whether interventions designed to 'raise it' actually work (Emler, 2001). As a measure of professional satisfaction it no doubt helps to counter the overly bureaucratic, economic, instrumental and target driven culture that adult learning has otherwise become. But it reflects a conservative and individualistic view of personal growth and social change: if you can't change the world or the political and economic trends over which you have no control, better change yourself to make the best of it! The government chooses to regard self esteem – rather than poverty or social class, for example – as both the cause and effect of social exclusion and welcomes any amount of short-term interventions designed to counter the dysfunctional and negative behaviour of those who do not have enough of it (Ecclestone, 2004). The belief that developing confidence and self- esteem can remedy a wide range of personal and social problems in turn acts to distract attention from the structural causes of sex inequality, institutional and actual racism and from the widening gap between rich and poor more generally. And of course, it plays to the prejudices of a profession that is already well used to labelling and stereotyping its students (Thompson, 2006).

The main problems with policies such as these can be summarised as follows:

- They rely on initiatives aimed at behaviour modification in increasingly coercive ways as the policy response to problems which are systemic or structural in nature.
- They utilise the kind of language and ideas that make learning sound more like therapy than education.
- The relentless onslaught of short-lived initiatives seem designed to keep people busy rather than educated via monumental amounts of paperwork.
- The obsession with measurable targets acts to divert the attention of practitioners away from the processes and outcomes of learning.

Time to use the F word . . .

The sight of Ruth Kelly, who at 36 was the youngest ever Secretary of State for Education, addressing the Labour Party Conference in Brighton in 2005, might suggest that women have come a long way in twenty years. Some would say that the energy, irreverence and political determination of second-wave feminism helped to clear the ground and pave the way for women like Kelly to find themselves in positions of political influence.

Somehow, I don't think it's a debt that Kelly would even recognise, let alone embrace. Feminism – the F word – is rarely spoken of in the corridors of power in contemporary Britain. For many younger women, those who have grown up with contraception on demand, legal abortion, less punitive divorce laws and a measure of choice when it comes to education, childbirth and employment, feminism is no longer the rallying cry it once was, so far as most women are concerned. The issues these days – for those who are thoughtful about the planet and the state of society – are more likely to be about global poverty, trade justice, the war in Iraq, climate change and their sense of cynicism and rage about politicians who do not listen, or who appear cavalier with the truth.

Party political research and recent opinion polls reveal a significant gender dimension when it comes to voting patterns and political activism. Women in greater numbers than men have stopped supporting the Labour government and are more likely than men to cite loss of trust, foreign policy and the war in Iraq as their reason for disaffection. In the general election of 2005 fewer women than men voted Conservative for the first time in the party's history. The leadership contest that soon followed was a decidedly macho affair, in which David Davis – the then front runner – paraded young women in tight T shirts with 'I'm a double D supporter' emblazoned on their chests, making it very clear that blokish sexism is alive and well beyond the football terraces.

What looks like progress concerning the general position of women in society, does not mean that everything is now alright – especially for women who are also poor, or elderly, or migrant workers, or from minority ethnic backgrounds. As we have seen, the fact that women consistently out-perform men in education has not yet opened the doors to equal pay for equal work, equal incomes, equal pensions, equal opportunities in the labour market, equality in decision-making or leadership roles. When it comes to political power, Ruth Kelly is still the exception rather than the rule. Only 27 per cent of Labour MPs are women.

Neither has progress towards equality done anything to diminish the sexual and domestic violence experienced by women. One in four violent crimes reported to the police each year is a crime of domestic violence. One woman – from all class, racial and ethnic backgrounds – is killed every three days by her violent partner. Every minute of every day, a woman somewhere in Britain calls the police to ask for help. Thirty per cent of all calls are from women who are pregnant. Thirty thousand children a year seek shelter in a refuge with their mothers who are on the run from violent men. This degree of violence costs employers £3 billion a year in sick leave, the criminal justice system £1 billion a year in legal costs, and the NHS and Social Services £1.5 billion a year in medical and other help. And these are just the statistics we know about. It is well known that huge numbers of women do not feel able – for a variety of reasons – to speak out about their experiences. In a political climate in which cruelty to foxes attracts more political attention than cruelty to women and children, it is economic arguments that have now replaced feminist arguments when it comes to persuading politicians to introduce legislation to take this matter seriously.

All of these are feminist concerns and should be everyone's concern. It is surprising that adult learning, relying as it does on large numbers of women as both front-line practitioners and learners for its very survival, remains quite so silent about the continuing oppression and discrimination faced by so many of those who are its students and its workforce. But it is less surprising in a political and educational climate in which what now counts as adult learning has been effectively stripped of any connection with its roots in the social and political struggle for social justice: what Raymond Williams called 'the long revolution' (McIlroy and Westwood, 1993); what feminists and socialists across the world have called liberation (Thompson, 1983; Finger and Asun, 2001; Walters and Manicom, 1996; Newman, 1994; Foley, 1999; Youngman, 2000); and what Bell Hooks and Freire have called 'the practice of freedom' (Hooks, 1994; Freire, 1972).

Ruth Kelly's speech in Brighton made use of a very different language and philosophy of purpose, to underline just what we have lost. Instead of an inspiring, wide-ranging celebration of creative, practical and intellectual engagement, linked to curiosity and pleasure, that once informed the liberal purpose of adult education. Or the concern to resource ordinary citizens in their urgent need for critical and reflexive understanding, in a complicated and troubled world, that once informed the radical purpose of adult education. Or the shared consciousness-raising, and life-changing curriculum innovations, that once inspired the feminist purpose of adult education. What Kelly outlined for the future sounded more like a threat than a promise and about as interesting and absorbing as the dark side of the moon.

Drafted, we presume, by an adviser at the DfES, and passed through Number 10 for approval, it may be unfair to yawn in the face of the messenger. But the commitment to 'every adult (having) the right to a lifetimes's opportunity of training' is hardly likely to save the planet or excite those who still imagine that education can open your mind, feed your passions, shift your life, change the way you see the world and add new knowledge and critical understanding to the sum total of human existence. Even in its own terms, it does nothing to address the sex inequalities that underpin the skills strategy or the gendered and racialised labour market which the strategy supports (Kelly, 2005).

In circumstances such as these, there are no prizes for guessing who has most to lose. When education becomes synonymous with this kind of learning, when learning becomes synonymous with training, when the economy becomes synonymous with the market and when training becomes the creature of the market, it's a lose-lose situation for everyone, especially those who have already been failed by the school system. All the talk about skills means that education gets lost. Information is confused with knowledge, competence is confused with understanding and learning at all levels is confused with its assessment. Training is presented as a technical and neutral operation which is good so long as it is marketable. If customers can't be found, the operation is closed down.

In this kind of climate, society loses because its members will become more ignorant, despite the threat of more and more training. And the bigger questions – to do with sex inequality and social justice, global poverty, political disaffection, violence against women, to name but a few – get increasingly ignored or reduced to platitudes and slogans. In the process, a society which knowingly persists in destroying the conditions on which it depends for its future – such as a challenging and expansive view of education – becomes the antithesis of a learning society.

References

Bowman, H., Colley, H. and Hodkinson, P. (2004) *Employability and Career Progression for Full time, UK resident Masters Students*, Interim Report, Manchester: Higher Education Career Support Unit.

Coote, A. and Campbell, B. (1982) *Sweet Freedom*, London: Picador

Department of Work and Pensions (2004) *Family Resources Survey Great Britain 2002–3*, London: DWP

DfES (1998) *The Learning Age: A Renaissance for a New Britain*, London: HMSO

DfES (2003) *21st Century Skills: Realising Our Potential*, Cm 5810, London: The Stationery Office

Ecclestone, K. (2004) 'Developing self esteem and emotional well-being – inclusion or intrusion?', *Adults Learning*, 16(3)

Eldred, J. *et al* (2005) 'Catching confidence', *Adults Learning*, 16(8)

Emler, N. (2001) *Self-Esteem: The Costs and Causes of Low Self Worth*, York: Joseph Rowntree Foundation

Equal Opportunities Commission (2005) *Britain's Hidden Brain Drain*, Manchester: EOC

Field, J (2000) *Lifelong Learning and the New Education Order*, Stoke-on-Trent: Trentham

Field, J. (2001) 'Lifelong learning and social inclusion', in Coffield, F. (ed), *What Progress are We Making with Lifelong Learning? – The evidence from research*, Newcastle: University of Newcastle

Finger, M. and Asun, J.M. (2001) *Adult Education at the Crossroads: Learning Our Way Out*, Leicester: Zed Books and NIACE

Foley, G. (1999) *Learning in Social Action: A Contribution to Understanding Informal Education*, Leicester: Zed Books and NIACE

Freire, P. (1972) *Pedagogy of the Oppressed*, Harmondworth: Penguin

Gray, J. (1992) *Men are from Mars, Women are from Venus*, Harper Collins

Hooks, B. (1994) *Teaching to Transgress: Education as the Practice of Freedom*, London: Routledge

Hyde, J.S. (2005) 'The gender similarities hypothesis', *American Psychologist*, 60(6)

James, O. (2005) 'From Venus and Mars', *The Guardian*, September 20th

Kelly, R. (2005) Speech to the Labour Party Conference, Brighton, September 2005

Learning and Skills Council (2005) *The Agenda for Change*, London: LSC

McGivney, V. (2004) *Men Earn Women Learn*, Leicester: NIACE

McGivney, V. (2005) *Adult Learning at a Glance*, Leicester: NIACE

McIlroy, J. and Westwood, S. (1993) *Border Country: Raymond Williams in Adult Education*, Leicester: NIACE

Newman, M. (1994) *Defining the Enemy: Adult Education in Social Action*, Sydney: Stewart Victor Publishing

ONS (2004) *Annual Survey of Hours and Earnings*, London: ONS

Pension Policy Institute (2003) *The Under-Pensioned Woman*

Rees, G., Fevre, R and Furlong, J (1997) 'History, place and the learning society: towards a sociology of lifetime learning', *Journal of Education Policy*, 12(6)

Spender, D. (1982) *Invisible Women: The Schooling Scandal*, London: Writers and Readers Publishing Cooperative

Thompson, J. (1983) *Learning Liberation: Women's Response to Men's Education*, London: Croom Helm

Thompson, J. (2006) 'Changing ideas and beliefs in lifelong learning', in Aspin, D. (ed) *Philisophical Perspectives on Lifelong Learning*, Springer

Thompson, J. with the Taking Liberties Collective (1989) *Learning the Hard Way: Women's Oppression in Men's Education*, London: Macmillan

Toynbee, P. (2005) 'Don't shrug off low pay', *The Guardian*, August 26th

Von Kotze, A. (2005) 'Are we all together?', *Adults Learning*, 16(10)

Walters, S. and Manicom, L. (eds) (1996) *Gender in Popular Education; Methods for Empowerment*, Zed Books and CACE

Westwood, S. (1984) *All Day Every Day: Factory and Family in the Making of Women's Lives*, London: Pluto

Women and Equality Unit (2004) *Individual Incomes of Men and Women 1996/7 to 2002/03*, London: DTI

Youngman, F. (2000) *The Political Economy of Adult Education and Development*, Leicester: Zed Books and NIACE

Chapter 4

Women and education in the South

Julia Preece

Introduction

Women's education in the South is premised on two struggles. A struggle against misrepresentation and a struggle for recognition. The misrepresentation starts with the title of this chapter and subsequent words associated with the South. The 'South' or Global South, as it is sometimes called, is a metaphor for those countries where statistical indicators for development are low. These indicators are usually identified by international aid agencies and include such figures as the number of people living on less than one or two USD$ a day, life expectancy ages, infant mortality rates, HIV/AIDS prevalence, illiteracy levels, gross domestic product per capita, unemployment and inflation rates. The Global South then is overwhelmingly defined in terms of its development deficiencies as measured by the dominant 'North' or Westernised countries. The countries of the South are often nations that were formerly colonised by European countries such as Britain, France and Spain. The way education is perceived, defined and promoted on a global scale is heavily influenced by those same European or Westernised discourses which provide most of the literature on education for women in the South.

This chapter starts, therefore, with a cautionary note. There is a growing body of literature which is reclaiming the pre-colonial educational heritage of formerly colonised nations and challenging their portrayal as static and 'unchanged since the Stone Age' (Kisian'ani, 2004, p.9). In terms of education it is argued that separate sets of traditions form the basis for particularly African or Asian worldviews (Avoseh, 2001; Said, 2003). These argue that traditional societies have always practiced indigenous pedagogies that embrace lifelong learning principles as foundations for active citizenship and nation building (Avoseh, 2001). In terms of gender, others demonstrate that colonial interference disrupted natural gender relations that were not necessarily built on Westernised notions of male dominance (Mulenga, 1999; Kunnie, 2000; Omolewa *et al*, 1998; Goduka, 2000). So Anfred *et al* (2004), for instance, argue that it is time gender research highlighted the myriad achievements of African men and women in education, art, music, agriculture, politics, economics and so on. Indeed Visvanathan (1997, p. 7) argues that the very use of the term development undermines the value base of non-European societies:

> The notion of development assumes the human ability to influence and control the natural and social environment. Static, agrarian societies may seek to live in harmony with the environment, but virtually every non-static society attempts to influence it.

Yet others, such as Snyder and Tadesse (1997), point out that women's present unequal share of the economy in developing countries is attributed in part to the colonial treatment of women as home-makers rather than farmers, thus bypassing their educational needs for taking part in a modern, technological and wage-based economy.

So the colonial period set the scene for present day unequal education and subsequent access to economic sustainability, with consequences for women's power sharing and participation in decision-making. Demand is now growing for context specific, culturally sensitive and relevant learning that recognises the indigenous knowledge and heritage of nations and their various ethnic groups. At the same time demand is also growing for the world to facilitate women's access to educational opportunities that will lead to women's equal participation in society at all levels. The remainder of this chapter addresses this latter concern in relation to policy issues, statistics and factors influencing women and girls' life chances in education.

Policy issues

The problem of North-South divisions starts with how lifelong learning is interpreted by international aid agencies. The tendency has been to set minimum basic education targets for the South (universal primary education), whilst surging forward with tertiary and continuing education strategies in the North:

> Lifelong learning actively adopted in the North while basic educa-
> tion is promoted in the South (often with narrow approaches . . .)
> means consolidating and deepening, rather than reducing the gap
> between North and South' (Torres, 2003, p. 144).

In other words, in a globalised world where high levels of literacy and
educational qualifications are a mechanism for recognition, engagement and
power sharing, all levels of educational achievement should be made not
only contextually relevant, but also accessible for everyone. An attempt to
redress the imbalance was made in Southern Africa, in 2003. The SADC[1]
Technical Committee for Education and Training took a broader vision for
lifelong learning than the largely instrumental, skills focused version for
Europe and in so doing went some way towards reflecting the opportunity to
embrace African value systems. The Committee's articulated primary goal
for lifelong education and training was: 'active democratic citizenship . . .
connecting individuals and groups to the structures of social, political and
economic activity in both local and global contexts' (Aitcheson, 2003,
p. 165). In spite of this effort to create a broad definition for lifelong learning,
in practice countries in the South (see Aitcheson, 2005 on South Africa for
example) continue to be manipulated through international aid agencies to
follow European models.

At the same time, women's organisations continue to campaign for a broader
understanding of gender-based needs that extend beyond internationally
designated minimum targets for girls' education. The plethora of such
organisations includes REPEM – the Latin American feminist movement;
FEMNET, The African Women's Development and Communication
Network; UNIFEM, the United Nations Development Fund for Women;
AWOMI – the African Women's Millennium Initiative on Poverty and
Human Rights; Nirantar, concerned with issues related to gender and
education in India; and DAWN, standing for Development Alternatives with
Women for a New Era.

The progress of these organisations and their initiatives is often hindered by
Western agendas that can hijack and overturn earlier progress on the
international stage. An example of decision-making processes over the past
five years in relation to women and education demonstrates this point.

CEDAW, the UN Convention on the Elimination of all forms of
Discrimination Against Women, was ratified in 1979 and signed up to by 173
countries by 2003. This agreement confirmed a commitment to educational

provision that extended beyond primary education, eliminated user fees, provided opportunities for non-formal education for women and girls, enhanced the quality of education, promoted infrastructure developments such as separate toilets, enhanced the content of education to eliminate gender biases and stereotypes. In support of this commitment the agreement also identified plans to compensate women and girls for burdens of home-based care, eliminate violence against women and ensure their rights to property and inheritance, provide meaningful livelihood and economic empowerment interventions (Voices rising, 2005). In other words, recognition that education is also about politics, power, attitudes and behaviour.

This convention was followed up in 1995 in Beijing at the 4th UN World Conference on Women. From this conference emerged the Beijing Declaration and Programme For Action (PFA). The PFA identified 12 critical areas of concern for women: poverty, education and training, health, violence, armed conflict, economy, decision making, institutional mechanisms, human rights, media, environment and the girl child (Asia Pacific GO Forum, 2004).

The PFA education goals were supported by the Dakar World Education forum in 2000 through the Dakar Framework for Action: Towards Education For All. Out of its six targets for 2015, four are specifically relevant to women's education:

- Ensure that the learning needs of all young people and adults are met through equitable access to appropriate learning and life skills programmes.
- Achieve a 50 per cent improvement in levels of adult literacy by 2015, especially for women, and equitable access to basic and continuing education for all adults.
- Eliminate gender disparities in primary and secondary education by 2005, achieve gender equality in education by 2015, with a focus on ensuring girls' full and equal access to and achievement in basic education of good quality.
- Improve all aspects of the quality of education and ensure excellence of all so that recognised and measurable learning outcomes are achieved by all, especially in literacy, numeracy and essential life skills.

In spite of the focus on women and adult education in these targets, however, the United Nations in 2000 set eight development targets, now known as the Millennium Development Goals (MDGs). These were adopted by international aid agencies and governments around the world and are less ambitious than the Beijing Declaration or the Education for All goals, particularly in relation to adults and specific women-driven agendas. As a result the complexity of structural, attitudinal and legal constraints to women's agency are hidden and women's issues are rendered invisible. Adult education is not a development goal at all.

The MDGs that are relevant to women and adults are:

- Poverty – the proportion of people living in extreme poverty in developing countries and the proportion of malnourished children should be reduced by at least one half between 1990 and 2015.
- Education – there should be universal primary education in all countries by 2015.
- Gender equality – progress toward gender equality and the empowerment of women should be demonstrated by eliminating gender disparity in primary and secondary education by 2015.

The MDGs are now driving international aid agendas and country poverty reduction strategies. At one level, such a high profile for development needs is to be welcomed. But the disadvantage is that developement targets that lie outside the specific indicators for the MDGs receive little or no attention. Few countries emphasise educational investment for poverty reduction, for instance. Non-formal education and adult illiteracy are given short shrift in country poverty reduction strategy papers (PRSPs) which are now produced by the poorest countries as a condition of aid. For example, out of 17 PRSPs that were checked for Education For All goals, whilst full primary education for all was highlighted in 15 papers, women's literacy was highlighted in only seven, and the elimination of gender disparity in only 7 (UNESCO IIEP, 2004). It is argued generally that a primary deficiency in the MDGs is their failure to adopt a human rights approach to development (Inter Press News Agency, 2005), which particularly affects women and minorities. Although the UN Millennium Task Force on Education and Gender Equality identified a further 12 indicators to monitor a broader range of priorities for empowering women (World Bank, 2005), these are not widely adopted by international aid agencies.

So what are the grounds for targeting women's needs more strongly in the South? And how should women's education be developed? The statistics present a gloomy picture, suggesting that there is much work to do.

Statistics

According to official statistics, of the 104 million children age 6–11 not in school, 60 million are girls. Nearly 40 per cent live in Sub Saharan Africa (SSA), 35 per cent in South Asia. At least 100 million girls will drop out of education before completing primary school (Herz and Sperling, 2004). Fifty-four countries (16 in SSA, 11 in East Asia and Pacific, seven in the Arab States) are at risk of not achieving gender parity in primary or secondary education by 2015. DFID (2000) also claims that only one or two per cent of children with disabilities receive education. When this level of education translates into adults who may be educated enough to sustain themselves, the prospects for adults who acquired their disability in childhood are meagre. Women with disabilities are perceived as bad risks so they do not get loans and experience stigma and discrimination in training opportunities (Lewis, 2004). These accumulated figures inevitably translate into adult illiteracy and other inequalities that affect men and women, but particularly women.

Of the 861 million illiterates in the whole world, 847 live in developing countries and two-thirds are women. The percentage of female adult illiterates in SSA is 61 per cent; in the Arab States 64 per cent; East Asia and Pacific 71 per cent; South and West Asia 61 per cent; Latin America and Caribbean 56 per cent. Participation rates in tertiary education in these areas are reduced to single figures (World Bank, 2005).

Children of uneducated mothers are more than twice as likely to die or be malnourished than children of mothers who have secondary or higher education (Save The Children, 2005). Yet each additional year of female education is thought to reduce child mortality by five to ten per cent. Women represent half of the 40 million people infected with HIV, but 57 per cent of positive HIV adults in Southern Africa.

Of the 534 million working poor, 60 per cent or more of women are in informal employment with meagre earnings, too low to raise people out of poverty. Women's work is poorly understood and measured and does not include unpaid care work. In developing countries it is women who support and care for families, grow food, collect fuel and water – but they are also the ones who face social and economic discrimination to prevent them from attending school, working for wages, taking part in civic life. Women held only 15 per cent of seats in national parliaments in 2003 around the world and account for only 20 per cent of students in engineering, manufacturing and construction. They hold one third or less of teaching posts in 16 SSA countries (EFA Global Monitoring Report, 2003).

To take just one country example, in Pakistan, where only 45 per cent of the population is literate, the literacy rate for women is only 32 per cent. In spite of progress in the last 59 years, 40 per cent of the population is categorised as living below the poverty line and only 60 per cent of girls enrol for schooling. Many services are poor and mortality rates are high. Poverty in Pakistan is on the increase, largely attributed to the high number of illiterate women (Attiqur-Rahman, 2005). Attiqur-Rahman cites a number of examples where programmes to increase literacy amongst women have had positive social and economic effects on people's lives. In spite of this evidence, she states that the public sector does not invest heavily in adult education, choosing to focus on primary education. She argues that this is a false economy, since 50 per cent of children drop out of school – mostly from families where the parents are illiterate.

It is commonly acknowledged that educated parents send their children to school. So it is a false economy not to focus on education for adults. Educated women participate in civic groups and political decision-making and have increased self-confidence. Girls with education have lower HIV infection rates, more knowledge about HIV, are more likely to seek medical care. When mothers have health care, education and economic opportunity, both they and their children have the best chance to survive and thrive. Educated women have a greater share of household income which results in a higher impact on child survival and children who are less likely to suffer from malnutrition. Educated mothers are more likely to immunise their children. Educated women are three times as likely as illiterate women to participate in political meetings and help rebuild communities after natural disasters. Other benefits include higher wages, reduced domestic violence and more productive farming (EFA Global Monitoring Report, 2003; Kabeer, 2005). In spite of these arguments for increasing access to education for women, they are visibly absent from current policy agendas.

Factors influencing women's and girls' life chances of education

A number of factors influence women's and girls' opportunities for education. They relate to poverty and sociocultural constraints such as household dynamics (such as son preference, the expectation in poor families that girls should look after siblings or supplement the family income), the power of tradition (such as early marriage), hidden domestic labours, vulnerability to HIV/AIDS, adding up the school bill. Enduring stereotypes (resulting in sexual violence and harassment that is responsible for underachievement and high drop-out rates) are exacerbated in adulthood. These include competing socio-economic constraints such as poverty and rural workloads, ignorance of women's human rights, gender power relations and abuse in the family and society (Adjamagbo-Johnson, 2004).

But it is also the concept of education itself which can exacerbate participation issues. Figueredo and Anzalone (2003) and Ramachandran (2003) point out that when education is available it is often irrelevant to people's daily lives; resources in terms of teachers and facilities are insufficient in number and quality; and even the calendar of the school year precludes participation when it clashes with rural workloads.

Where initiatives targeted at women do exist they are often inappropriate. On the one hand policy makers often continue to see the benefits of educating girls and women simply in terms of improving family health and welfare, rather than preparing women for a more equal place in the economy and in society (Hogg *et al*, 2005). On the other hand income-generating initiatives that do exist are provided without an education component that addresses women's structural inequalities in society – such as access to loans or credit.

Parthasarathy *et al* (forthcoming) discuss how micro credit has been promoted as a 'magic bullet' strategy for development. Yet schemes create minimum opportunity for women to acquire knowledge of production processes. So partial education that addresses the mechanics of credit systems does not address the consequential poverty resulting from gender disparities in legal access to savings, nor does it address the income poverty levels of women in micro enterprises who often simply become another form of exploited labour. The de-contextualised nature of their micro credit education has meant that women continue to be disempowered and women remain on the edge of the production chain.

So for many women microfinance per se has limited impact. Poverty reduction and empowerment goals are therefore a necessary integral component of programme design for women's education (Parthasarathy *et al*, forthcoming; Lewis, 2004)

Walingo (forthcoming) provides evidence to show that in Kenya poor adult education training amongst agriculture demonstrators means they are not able to understand the learning needs of poor women who receive development input regarding food security initiatives. Women with low initial education need additional educational input to integrate their livestock input with knowledge of nutrition, production improvement methods, food processing and preservation. Walingo argues that general education is not enough to support the necessary skills development for women to move themselves out of subsistence level farming.

Similarly, disaster management strategies in response to war or earthquakes can miss educational opportunities. Menon and Godbole (2004) report that few development initiatives integrate life skills and consciousness-raising education in these situations. Poor households have a smaller chance of overcoming disaster because they are already weakened by malnutrition, inadequate healthcare and lower levels of schooling. Post-disaster initiatives, poverty-alleviation programmes and education are usually treated separately by policy makers.

Literacy

Education policies designed by international agencies and national governments often focus on literacy. Policies are based on the premise that universal literacy can accelerate national development and reduce the dependency of emerging economies on Western resources (World Bank, 1988). Egbo (2000) argues, however, that the issue of literacy is not that simple. It can mean different things to different people. Literacy alone does not seem to change women's economic status for instance. She argues for something more – a 'critical literacy' that would stimulate women to recognise and question the sources of their oppression.

Equally Menon and Godbole (2004) report that when adult education in India is confined to basic literacy with little support for post literacy, this results in a relapse back into illiteracy, which affects further life chances for skills updating or advancement. Since low wages are often linked to poor literacy levels and out-of-date skills, a continuing diet of low-level education opportunities perpetuates the cycle of relative and absolute income poverty.

What works?

Although literacy constitutes a major part of adult education in developing countries this picture actually misrepresents the nature of adult education generally and the nature of women's education. It has long been argued that adult education is provided through a variety of media and organisations, for many of which adult education is not their core business (Preece and Singh, 2005). The nature of adult education embraces concepts of empowerment, participation, drawing on learner experience and building capacity to challenge inequalities. Women's education is most effective when it draws on these concepts and addresses societal structural inequalities as well as practical skills. The most innovative and gender sensitive practices are undertaken by multi-sectoral programmes and civil society organisations. They may focus on a particular issue but often result in addressing other issues, sometimes as unintended outcomes (Hogg, 2005). A few examples are cited here.

Literacy evaluators and researchers now advocate a 'literacy second' approach – where classes work around the common interests of people, then identify how literacy and numeracy can further the participants' development needs and interests (Oxenham, 2004).

REFLECT was developed by ActionAid as an alternative participatory programme aimed to increase people's confidence in their own knowledge so as to enhance their acting on it. The idea was to assist people in controlling and shaping literacy, where discussion of local contexts would facilitate a bottom up programme of development at local levels. Whilst Fiedrich and Jellema (2003) suggest that empowerment as an outcome of these programmes is often exaggerated and still driven by external agendas, others have claimed significant improvements in a curriculum approach that begins with the context of women's lives.

Parajuli and Enslin (1990), for instance, describe how in Nepal critical pedagogical practices can play a part in developing women's social movements. Literacy classes use key words that address women's concerns such as lack of recognition of women's work, men's card playing, drinking and violence, scarcity of wood for firemaking. They claim that these classes gave women the courage to initiate concrete steps to ameliorate them. Women created a song about these concerns and began to question, during literacy discussions, the concept of development and cultural practices that disempowered women. This resulted in collective actions to campaign for women's spaces and improve their lives. The strength was in the classes' regeneration of the history and culture of the participants: 'Literacy provided a forum in which local memories of women's power and subordination in the past shaped the struggle for survival and identity in the present' (Parajuli and Enslin, 1990, p. 54).

An example of a multi-agency approach through local voluntary organisations in Andra Pradesh is described by Pant (2004). Here the goal of strengthening women's self esteem, analytical skills, competencies and consciousness drove a capacity-building skills development programme. It included study tours, hands-on training, demonstrations, discussions and exposure to new ideas within a women-friendly enabling environment. The outcomes included both cognitive and behavioural changes in the form of attitudes and styles of communication. Women now actively participate and challenge injustices, using their literacy and numeracy skills. They send their children to school, and have increased their bargaining power in the family. The programmes enabled women to form a collective identity, resulting in enhanced abilities to negotiate with government officials and outsiders, and achievement of practical outcomes such as access to their own savings.

Von Kotze (2005) describes how community health clubs, through health education and promotion materials, created networks of solidarity in Sierra Leone by adopting a rights-based approach to education. The education sessions encouraged questions like: 'What are the relationships of power between people in this situation and who has what duties to ensure that everyone's rights to live with dignity are safeguarded?' (p. 15). Weekly meetings end with decisions for particular activities to be undertaken during the week. Participants are encouraged to construct new understandings by examining their experiences in relation to new information:

> Rural people can transform their well-being and health status once they organise and mobilise with a sense of common purpose. When participants make broader connections between symptoms of sickness, individual actions, social taboos and cultural habits, and the lack of health care provision, their collective resolve can lead to pressures on local authorities and, eventually on the state (p. 16).

Education that addresses income poverty amongst adults is often non-formal. That is, vocational skill training centres may target rural or otherwise disadvantaged people. Sandhaas (2004) cites an EXPRO[2] programme in Ethiopia. This takes a livelihoods approach, combining vocational skills and literacy training, to disaffected young females, alongside participatory methodologies through a multisectoral approach to capacity building and awareness raising. Training programmes are devised in consultation with many stakeholders and linked to credit resources that support small enterprise start ups.

Environmental awareness is promoted through a permaculture project in the Philippines that aims to promote love of nature as well as demonstrate the economic sustainability of small-scale farming through increased practical knowledge reinforced by experience and example. The key feature here is a collective, co-operative approach to living in harmony with the planet (Dy, 2004).

These schemes and others similar to this often use literacy as the basis for their work but through a life skills and livelihoods approach to developing social awareness and knowledge of how to engage with service providers. Reading materials are developed around topics such as health and nutrition, income generation, environment promotion, women's development, society and culture, child rights, child and women trafficking and prevention, water and sanitation (Alam, 2004).

Adaptation and flexibility are key to these approaches, so that new technologies also can be applied in a way that is relevant and useful. Torres (2003), for instance, cites the adaptation of computers into low cost and low literacy touch screen resources for people in India and Brazil.

At the other end of the scale universities are providing educational programmes that engage with adult education as a discipline in its own right, often addressing 'gender' as a cross cutting issue across the curriculum (Department of Adult Education in Botswana for instance). University Departments are also building scholarship in women's issues and concepts of lifelong learning (University of the Western Cape, Pakistani Women's Universities, for example). The international networks and organisations mentioned earlier in this chapter provide a forum for global exchanges in relation to development issues and they create platforms for women's voices to be heard on a global as well as local scale.

Achievements in changing the status quo, however, rely on political will and legislative change. The most successful environments for holistic, multisectoral educational approaches are usually supported by institutional legal frameworks and facilitating mechanisms, such as an Education Act, Education Encouragement Fund, relevant basic education curricula, and country comprehensive poverty reduction and growth strategies (UNESCO IIEP, 2002, pp. 37–43).

Summary

Many of the challenges for women's education in the South mirror the challenges for women around the world. They include the need to change systems and power structures, laws, political processes, administrative structures and procedures that marginalise or discriminate against women. Educational approaches that include gender sensitive curricula that challenge patriarchal, violent masculinity and promote positive sexual identities enable women's awareness to be raised about the structures around them that contribute to their disempowerment. Once awareness is raised, then the women are supported in finding a voice to challenge the systems that created their impoverishment. Addressing these political issues will include tackling the reasons that force girls to drop out of school, such as violence, sexual harassment and care burdens (UK Gender and Development Network, 2005). But on top of this, legal structures and practices that protect women's land rights, labour rights, agricultural activities, livelihoods and traditional knowledge, are all infrastructure necessities that will enable women to access and benefit from educational opportunities.

References

Adjamagbo-Johnson, K. (2004) 'From Beijing to Addis Ababa: what progress for African women?' *Pambazuka News*. http://www.pambazuka.org/index.php?id=24944 accessed 12 March 2005

Aitcheson, J. (2003) 'Adult literacy and basic education: a SADC regional perspective', *Adult Education and Development*, 60: 161–170.

Aitcheson, J. (2005) 'Lifelong learning in South Africa: dreams and delusions', *International Journal of Lifelong Education*, 23(6): 575–516

Alam, K.R. (2004) 'Ganokendra – an innovative model for poverty alleviation', *Adult Education and Development*, 63: 155–166

Attiqur-Rahman, S. (2005) 'Poverty and adult education: the experience in Pakistan', in Preece, J. and Singh, M. (eds) *Adult Learning and Poverty Reduction*, Hamburg: UNESCO UIE, pp. 30–36

Avoseh, M. B. M. (2001) 'Learning to be active citizens: lessons of traditional Africa for lifelong learning', *International Journal of Lifelong Education*, 20: 479–486

Department for International Development (2000) *Disability Poverty and Development*, London: DFID

Dy, E. E. (2004) 'Community awareness services for ecological concern (CASEC)', Philippines, in Preece, J. (ed) *Adult Education and Poverty Reduction: A Global Priority*. Conference proceedings June 14–16, pp. 18–85, http://www.gla.ac.uk/centres/cradall/pr_botswana.shtm

Egbo, M. (2000) *Gender, Literacy and Life Chances in Sub Saharan Africa*, Clevedon: Multilingual Matters

EFA Global Monitoring Report (2003) *Gender and Education for All. Summary Report*, Paris: UNESCO

Fiedrich, M. and Jellema, A. (2003) *Literacy, Gender and Social Agency: Adventures in Empowerment*, Research Report for Action Aid UK

Figueredo, V. and Anzalone, S. (2003) *Alternative Models for Secondary Education in Developing Countries: Rationale and Realities*. American Institute for Research in collaboration with The Academy for Educational Development, University of Pittsburg: Juarez and Associates Inc

Goduka, I. N. (2000) 'African/indigenous philosophies: legitimizing spiritually centred wisdoms within the academy', in Higgs, P., Vakalisa, N. C. G., Mda, T.V. and Assie-Lumumba, N.T. (eds) *African Voices in Education*, Lansdowne, SA: Juta, pp. 63–83

Herz, B. and Sperling, G. B. (2004) *What Works in Girls Education?* New York: Council on Foreign Relations

Hogg, A. (2005) 'Finding a curriculum that works under trees: literacy and health education for adolescent girls in rural Malawi', *Development in Practice*, 15(5): 655–667

Inter Press News Agency (2005) 'Millennium development goals: glossing over women's issues' http://ipsnews.net/news.asp?idnews=30019 accessed September 2005

Kisian'ani, E. N. W. (2004) 'Decolonising gender studies in Africa', in Arnfred, S., Bakare-Yusef, B., Kisian'ani, E. W., Lewis, D., Oyewumi, O., Steady, F.C. (contributors) *African Gender Scholarship*, Senegal: CODESRIA, pp. 9–26

Kunnie, J. (2000) 'Indigenous African philosophies and socioeducational transformation in 'post-apartheid' Azania', in Higgs, P., Vakalisa, N.C.G., Mda, T.V. and Assie-Lumumba, N.T. (eds) *African Voices in Education*, Lansdowne, S. A.: Juta, pp. 158–178

Lewis, C. (2004) 'Microfinance from the point of view of women with disabilities', *Gender and Development*, 12(1): 28–39

Menon, G. and Godbole, P. (2004) 'Programming adult education in a post-earthquake area: CARE experiences with adolescent girls in Kutch', in Preece, J. (ed) *Adult Education and Poverty Reduction: A Global Priority*. Conference proceedings June 14–16, pp. 18–85, http://www.gla.ac.uk/centres/cradall/pr_botswana.shtm

Mulenga, D. (1999) 'Reflections on the practice of participatory research in Africa', *Convergence*, 32: 33–46

Omolewa, M., Adeola, O. A., Adekanmbi, G. A., Avoseh, M. B. M. and Braimoh, D. (1998) *Literacy, Tradition and Progress*, Hamburg: UNESCO Institute for Education

Oxenham, J. (2004) 'ABET vs Poverty: What have we learned?', *Adult Education and Development*, 63: 83–102

Pant, M. (2004) 'Adult education and livelihood: women as agents of change', *Adult Education and Development*, 63: 121–144

Parajuli, P. and Enslin, E. (1990) 'From learning literacy to regenerating women's space', *Convergence*, XXIII(1): 44–55

Parthasarathy, S. K., Sharma, J., Dwivedi, A. (forthcoming) 'Women's education, empowerment and micro credit: making the connections', in Preece, J., van der Veen, R. and Raditloaneng, W. N. (ed) *Adult Education and Poverty Reduction: Issues for Research Policy and Practice*, Gaborone: Lentswe La Lesedi

Preece, J. and Singh, M. (eds) (2005) *Adult Learning and Poverty Reduction*, Hamburg: UNESCO UIE

Preece, J., van der Veen, R. and Raditloaneng, W. N. R. (forthcoming) *Adult Education, Lifelong Learning and Poverty Reduction*, Leicester: NIACE

Ramachandran, V. (2003) Backward and Forward Linkages that Strengthen Primary Education *INDIASOCIAL.ORG. www.epw.org.in/*

Said, E. (2003) *Orientalism: Western Conceptions of the Orient*, Harmondsworth: Penguin

Sandhaas, B. (2005) 'Community based non-formal livelihood skills training for youth and adults in selected regions of Ethiopia (EXPRO)', *Adult Education and Development*, 64: 47–64

Save The Children (2005) *State of the World's Mothers 2005: The Power and Promise of Girls Education*, Westport, Connecticut: Save the Children

Snyder, M. and Tadesse, M. (1997) 'The African context: women in the political economy', in Visvanathan, N. *et al* (eds) *The Women, Gender and Development Reader*, London: Zed Books, pp. 75–78

Kabeer, N. (2005) 'Gender equality and women's empowerment: a critical analysis of the third Millennium Development Goal', in Sweetman, C. (ed) *Gender and the Millennium Development Goals*, Oxford: Oxfam

Torres, R.M. (2003) 'Lifelong Learning: a new momentum and a new opportunity for adult basic learning and education (ABLE) in the South', *Adult Education and Development*, Supplement to 60, p. 240

von Kotze, A. (2005) 'Are we all together?', *Adults learning*, 15(10): 14–16

UK Gender and Development Network (2005) *Analysis of the Commission for Africa Report*. www.gadnetwork.org

UNESCO International Institute for Educational Planning (2002) Untitled Paper for the interagency strategic group meeting on lifelong learning. Hamburg, organised by UNESCO Institute for Education

UNESCO IIEP (2004) *Education and the PRSPs. A Review of Experiences*, Unesco Institute for Education Planning www.unesco.org/iiep

UNIFEM (2005) *News Release*, August http://www.unifem.org/news_events/story_detail.php?StoryID=295 accessed 7 September 05

Voices Rising (2005) Gender and GCAP (Africa). *Voices Rising*, Year III Vol. 3, no. 142, June.

Walingo, M. K. (forthcoming) 'Efficacy of education in the advancement of agricultural projects for food security and poverty reduction in Kenya', in Preece, J. (eds) *Adult Education and Poverty Reduction: A Global Priority*. Conference proceedings June 14–16, pp. 18–85, http://www.gla.ac.uk/centres/cradall/pr_botswana.shtm

Visvanathan, N. (1997) 'General introduction', in Visvanathan, N., Duggan, L., Nisonoff, L. and Wiegersma, N. (eds) *The Women, Gender and Development Reader*, London: Zed Books

World Bank (1988) *Education in Sub Saharan Africa: Policies for Adjustment*, Washington DC: World Bank

World Bank (2005) World Development Indicators http://www.worldbank.org/data/wdi2005/wditext/Section2_1.htm accessed 24th october 2005

Notes

1. SADC stands for the Southern African Development Community with a membership of 13 countries: Angola, Botswana, Democratic Republic of Congo, Lesotho, Malawi, Mauritius, Mozambique, Namibia, South Africa, Swaziland, United Republic of Tanzania, Zambia and Zimbabwe.
2. An extra programme of IIZ/DVV's regular country programme with special funds from the German Ministry for Economic Cooperation and Development (BMZ).

Chapter 5
A gift in their hands[1]

Wilma Fraser, Chris Scarlett and Annie Winner

Imagine, if you will, the unexceptional scene. It is February 1903, and in a modest house in Clapham Common, South London, a young married couple are sitting at their kitchen table. He is a cashier in the local Co-operative Society, and is urging his case with the familiar passion which characterises his engagement with the world. She is listening, occasionally interjecting; she agrees with him but knows the time and effort that would be involved. Their son is only two years old and his father would be away from home so much. Finally, Frances reaches into her purse and brings out half a crown (12.5p). Handing it to Albert, she pronounces him 'Honorary Secretary' (pro-tem), and the Association to Promote the Higher Education of Working Men is born. The 'unexceptional' has become the exceptional; the Association would be publicly launched in August of that year at a meeting in Oxford, and the name of Albert Mansbridge would be written in history as the founder of the largest voluntary movement for adult education in Britain. What we know of Frances is largely restricted to that single act of domestic sacrifice.

We are not suggesting that Albert in any way sought to underplay the contribution of his wife. On the contrary, his relations with women were probably stamped with the same respect he accorded his mother, who, as an active member of the local Women's Co-operative Guild, had taught him much about the 'ethical ideals and voluntary self-help of Co-operation that made it such a strong and distinctive working-class movement' (Alfred, 1987). But the simplicity of Frances's act, and the profundity of its consequences, seems somehow emblematic of the untold and, literally, innumerable gifts of domestic sacrifice which women have always made for men, and without which the public realm could be neither sustained nor enhanced. Gifts in their hands, indeed.

In 1905, the Association changed its name to the Workers' Educational Association (WEA), 'partly' as Marsh (2000) notes 'due to pressure from the Women's Co-operative Guild'. Marsh continues as follows:

> This was not inappropriate, since 'not only Albert Mansbridge but others of his colleagues were sustained in their tasks by the devotion and self-sacrifice of their wives'.

This familiar story of the nourishment of the public sphere by the 'devotion' of women in the private and domestic is so axiomatic it requires no further elaboration here. Our task in this chapter is to concentrate on the challenges which women's education in the WEA has both posed and endured throughout its history thus far, and to note the interplay between the rise and falling fortunes of women's education in the Association – and indeed within the more general educational ideologies of the wider world – with the broader socio-political discourses which form and inform that interaction.

The first problem is one of definition; 'women's education' is generally taken to mean 'education by and for women'. However, the slogan, whilst having a certain declamatory ring, assumes homogeneity in both curricular content and delivery which can be profoundly misleading. The concept of 'women's education' has always been contested, and its provision and articulation have rendered it subject to attack from both the left and the right. In this sense, Benn's broader analysis of women's education in Britain in the nineteenth and twentieth centuries might also be used to describe its articulation within the microcosm of the WEA (Benn, 1996).

> [Women's education] could alternatively be categorised as relativist, where women are only seen in relation to others, particularly their husbands and children; compensatory, where women's disadvantage can be overcome by incorporating them into existing structures and norms; liberal, with its emphasis on individual development and limited social reform; or radical, where education is seen as a site for collective action and social change.

The idea that women should require an exclusive space in which to pursue their studies and explore their experiences is equally problematic. On the one hand, it is consistent with a radical agenda seeking to analyse and challenge the socio-economic discourses which have contained and constrained women as 'the other'. This assumes a fundamental similarity which extends beyond class, race and differences of sexual orientation. On the other hand, demanding a separate space for an already marginalised section of the population occasioned further opportunities for exclusion or containment. However, for all its inadequacies, for our purposes, women's education defined as 'by and for women' will have to do, although perhaps the following takes us a little further towards a definition for the WEA:

> To be effective Women's Education must be rooted in and shaped by women's lived experience – historical and current, personal and collective. In working to engage the full capacities of all students it seeks to combine clarity and excitement of thought and theory with attention to feelings, circumstances and the boundaries which circumvent women's lives. (WEA, 1989, p. 6)

So far as we know from the evidence that survives, the early years of the WEA were marked by an interesting shift towards addressing the 'special' needs of women. In 1909, a Women's Department was established and, in 1910, Alice Wall was appointed as its first, paid, woman's officer on the condition that her salary was generated from outside mainstream funds (Munby, 2003). Also in 1910, a meeting was convened in Reading at which 'Miss Alice Wall, from the London headquarters, urged the development of a women's section and special classes for women' (Hinder, unknown). In a wonderful example of the domestic sphere segueing into the public arena, Alice Wall's appeal resulted in a survey, the outcome of which was to arrange for the most popular choice, a 'stitchery' class to be established. No fewer than seventy women turned up, which 'provided great opportunity for talk and discussion . . . leading to a new venture – Lectures on Public Procedure and Local Government' (Hunter and Clarke, 2003).

With women's suffrage an increasingly burning issue, in the years leading up to World War One, 1912 saw the publication of *Women in the Workers' Educational Association* urging equality in the struggle for social improvement. It carried the name of Ida Hony, although it was probably written by Alice Wall before she left the Association, as was required, when she married (Munby, 2003, p. 67):

> If the WEA is to gain any substantial victory in its campaign against ignorance and injustice, men and women must be fighting side by side . . . Neither party can march by itself without endangering both its own safety, and that of the party it has left, and if one ceases to make progress, the other is held back too; so, of all the special efforts the WEA has to make

today, perhaps none is more important than the special effort it is making on behalf of women. (Aird, 1982)

In the roller-coaster ride which was to characterise the fortunes of women's education throughout the WEA's first hundred years, 1916 saw 'this initiative for women-only classes [lapse] due to the non-replacement of the National Women's Officer and the collapse of the Women's Advisory Committee' (Benn, 1996, p. 381).

Full suffrage for women was finally achieved in 1928, the same year that a WEA leaflet described its 'opportunities for women' which included single lectures, short courses, classes of longer duration, and weekend and summer schools, as follows:

In all the classes the method adopted is not that of going back to school, but rather that of a joint adventure to find out more about things in which the class members are interested, and to discover what ideas other people have about these things. (WEA, 1928)

The notion of 'special' provision for women is evident in another 1928 publication, a report on tutor training:

If educational work is to be properly developed among women, attention must be given to educational propaganda and to the provision of special women's classes in the more elementary stages. For these classes, women are on the whole more suitable than men. (Carnegie UK Trustees, 1928)

When we reach the 1940s, we find the WEA again providing for women during the Second World War in the hostels of women munitions workers, the Women's Land Army and the Women's Timber Corps:

The tutors ... feel that the course has been one of the most enjoyable and useful in which they have ever taken part. We have nothing but admiration for girls who, after a hard and dirty day's threshing, reach the hostel at 6.30pm, rush for their meal, wash and change in order to get in late to a class. (WEA, 1994)

Perhaps the tone of these extracts seems patronising today. However words such as 'adventure' and 'discovery', and the idea of enthusiastic 'rushing' to get to a class after a hard day's physical labour, conjure up considerably more excitement and purpose than is apparent in some more contemporary educational literature.

Once the war was over and men and women were returned to their 'proper jobs' in a gendered labour market and a sharply differentiated public and private sphere, the 1950s, predictably, saw the reintroduction of courses for working-class women that concentrated on the domestic side of life (Benn, 1996, pp. 384–5). There were, of course, broader educational opportunities for middle-class women, and during the decade the WEA's partnerships with such organisations as the Women's Co-operative Guild, the Townswomen's Guild and the Women's Institute continued to thrive. The consolidation of this more liberal, and reformist, space characterised the delivery of much general adult education for the next fifty years; to a student body comprised mostly of women, the majority of whom would neither recognise nor countenance the seismic shifts which the new decade would bring.

However, enough of them must have been sufficiently influenced by the feminist zeitgeist to press for similarly radical changes in women's education in the WEA. Protest against the war in Vietnam, Civil Rights, student activism, the growth of the Campaign for Nuclear Disarmament (CND) and the Peace Movement more generally, all contributed in the West, at least, to the emergence of the New Left. This, in turn, acted as the backdrop in the 1960s and 1970s to the re-emergence of second-wave feminism in the guise of the Women's Liberation Movement. The challenge was both epistemo-logical as well as political. Women's Liberation demanded the radical deconstruction of patriarchal ways of knowing, as well as being, and the WEA was at the forefront of this process. Women's Studies courses flour-ished in ways that were both academically radical and politically in touch with more grassroots demands for individual and collective empowerment, as the following declamation articulates: 'We are not about joining the world. We are about re-shaping the world' (WEA, 1989, p. 6).

The most striking aspect of this claim, made by a woman in a women's education workshop in the 1980s, is the lack of irony attending its declara-tion. This was a decade marked by an easy alliance between the medium and the message, which a reminiscent trawl through a few tin and plastic badges illustrates: 'For a Reagan-free Caribbean', 'Support the Greenham women', both demands underlined by another simple assertion that 'I didn't vote Tory'. Such confident sloganising may now seem, in a world that has grown weary and cynical about politics, as refreshingly activist if somewhat naive. Yet the fact that such statements could be made, never mind so roundly declaimed, takes us back to a period where belief in the power to effect change, indeed to 'reshape the world' found enthusiastic expression, and support, in the WEA. This is not to suggest that the WEA's embrace of women's education was ever sufficiently wholehearted to meet these radical challenges, yet the 1980s saw a significant shift in attitude and articulation as the following WEA 1987 Conference Resolution 33 testifies:

> This Conference applauds the development and achievements of the WEA's Women's Education programmes . . . this Conference requests that the NEC set up a working group in Women's Education to evaluate the position at this time and to suggest policy and resourcing for the future development of this vital area of work. (WEA, 1989, p. 4)

Much had happened in the intervening twelve years since the formation of a National Women's Advisory Group in 1977. This became the National Women's Education Advisory Committee (WEAC) in 1980, empowered to link with representatives in each geographical district to form a network and to consolidate the development of women's education, including curriculum delivery. In 1985, the WEA appointed a fourth National Officer at the highest level of the organisation whose responsibilities included developing and supporting women's education, a post made 'permanent' in 1987. Between 1984 and 1989, the highly regarded series of pamphlets entitled *Breaking our Silence* was published. In May 1984, the WEA published the first in a new series of the *Women's Studies Newsletter*. Its aims included:

- (Acting) as a forum for debate and discussion on women's education both within and outside the WEA.
- (Increasing) understanding of the principles and practices of women's education.

Key curriculum developments were encapsulated and encouraged by the publication of resource packs such as *Getting Started* and *Women and Health*, both taking as their starting point the 'assumption that the personal is the political' (WEA, 1989, p. 7). These included *Return to Learn* and *New Opportunities for Women* programmes, all articulated within the same overriding adherence to the key tenets and principles of a more radical approach to women's education.

This is not to say that the 1980s represented a golden age either. Thatcherism was in its political ascendancy and the policies, values and practices of the

New Left were increasingly in retreat, and the WEA has never provided a neutral or constant backdrop against which social and individual currents battle or hold sway. The movement, like everything else, was formed and informed by broader socio-economic drivers and imperatives than the personalities and political groupings which competed for attention within its domain. Accusations of generating 'apartheid education' mingled with some grudging acceptance that women-only courses were okay 'only if they (could) be seen as a kind of confidence-raising springboard into "real", that is mixed education' (WEA, 1989, p. 6). The arguments were often fierce and did not always result in the policy and implementation decisions we might have hoped for. But at least the debates took place and involved strong arguments about both politics and purpose. The difference in terms of the contested discourses available to women is, nonetheless, highly salutary when compared with the narrow focus and monocular vision of current educational delivery in 2005.

Giving voice to the personal in relation to the political was regarded as challenging the authoritarianism of the masculinist left, whilst articulating a different kind of collective potential. Women sought to express themselves in language and actions proclaiming meaningful and connected agency in the world, and the WEA provided some space for such agency to develop. The tumultuous political landscape of the 1980s encouraged reference to the radical potential of learning, and women's education claimed its share of these rebellious acres. Despite the drift of Thatcher's neo-liberal individualism (or perhaps because of it) women sought and fought, often with each other, for a means of finding connectivity in difference.

> The problem is that the thrust of recent Government funding policies, with their emphasis on simply determined cost-effectiveness, may serve to push Women's Education and other areas of innovative WEA work more and more to the margins. (WEA, 1989, p. 5)

As the 1990s dawned, these words proved chillingly prescient. When the National Officer with responsibility for Women's Education left the WEA at the start of the 1990s, she was not replaced, and the national focus and support for women's education became seriously compromised. The language of empowerment was hijacked by the empty rhetoric of the market place, and education's transformative potential began to be harnessed and corralled by the culture of learning outcomes, accreditation, progression routes, and added value:

> Informal women's education is probably at least as responsive
> and wide-ranging as any conventional provision but it is
> extremely difficult to fit into conventional management tools
> such as target setting, three-year planning cycles and the like.
> (Scarlett and Winner, 1995)

By the 1990s, there was no longer any question that feminism and matters of
gender equality were in retreat in Britain. Some significant improvements in
a few specific areas of women's lives were enough to fuel the convenient view
that women had 'caught up' with men (see Chapter 3, this volume). Not
surprisingly, but regrettably, the WEA mirrored the wider world. Women
predominated as students, part-time tutors and volunteers, but men dominated
the senior management positions. Female WEA staff, working with women in
local communities on a daily basis, knew the lie in the rhetoric, yet struggled
to justify their work in the increasingly hostile and financially precarious
climate.

However, the feminist blaze was still smouldering in the WEA, and a group
of activists marshalled their resources to get a resolution passed at the 1993
Biennial Conference to establish a Women's Education Committee (WEC),
and to urge the reinstatement of the post of National Officer.

A key factor in the success at conference was the existence of the Margaret
James bequest, a fund then totalling over £90,000, which had been specifically left to the Association in 1943 to provide scholarships to support the
university education of working-class women. The Charity Commissioners
broadened this remit to one of promoting women's education more generally.
Who would oversee the deployment of this considerable sum? A Women's
Education Committee (WEC) was established to manage the disbursement of
the fund, and a committed and proven member of staff was appointed as
Secretary to the Committee on a 0.5 basis to ensure operational efficiency
and minimise managerial challenge. In 2001, she was given a full-time post
as National Co-ordinator of Women's Education.

WEC, duly constituted, started work. It was a struggle at first. Women at the
grassroots were generally delighted at the emergence of this new committee,
whilst WEC members were conscious of the double-edged nature of their
responsibilities. Had they accepted a poisoned chalice? Would they provide
the WEA with a spurious legitimacy in some educational circles; a respect for
its commitment to women's education that was, in reality, as conflicted as
ever? In the end, pragmatism prevailed, but WEC members knew from the

start that their days were numbered. The then General Secretary had insisted that the legacy be spent in its entirety (rather than just disbursing the income from the fund) so it was decided to spend it in such a way that women's education would be firmly enough embedded in the districts to remain vibrant and connected to local communities long after the bequest, and WEC, had gone.

High quality course materials were seen as a priority, and five national women's education courses were produced. WEC wanted the courses to both reflect the WEA tradition of student-centred education, the feminist tradition of women-centred education, and also to provide a challenge to the atomised, instrumental, individualised learning now firmly in the ascendant elsewhere. As we have seen, there has always been a tension within women's education between empowering the individual or the collective; between education as compensatory or radical. As Jean Barr had noted in 1984, 'starting from where people are is an excellent starting point but a lousy finishing point. It can often leave them there' (Barr, 1984).

The curriculum was intended to articulate the 'personal as political' by providing a generic course, *The Women's Learning Programme*, which would acknowledge individual need whilst bridging its expression to an understanding of the collective. And so, whilst including topics such as women's health and women's history, it also offered a follow-on course where groups of women worked collectively and still gained credit. It proved to be highly successful, and over the years, with various re-writes and updates, it provided women-centred education for thousands of students.

A second course on women and domestic violence was developed with Women's Aid. It offered some volunteer training as well as insights into the issues affecting one in four women in Britain today. Recruitment to the course proved troublingly problematic. Despite targeting women currently uninvolved in any personal domestic violence, it soon became clear that no such line could be drawn. Women often move in and out of a cycle of abuse and this tragic pattern presented tutors with some of their most challenging work, requiring the establishment of a support network and helpline for those tutoring the course.

Other national courses quickly followed: Women and Health; a tutor training programme for self-defence tutors; and a programme of courses aimed at women trade unionists and recruited through UNISON, some of whose women's officers gave invaluable expertise and support to the work. The residential weekend schools run through the UNISON Women, Work and Society programme were electric and life-changing for the significant number of women who attended them.

Whilst curriculum development was at the heart of WEC's work, much was achieved in other areas. Through the re-establishment of a contacts network, a development fund gave support to informal outreach activities which often led to courses or, in some cases, more women's branches; an annual Women's Education Residential Weekend was organised which brought WEA women together from all over the UK. International work included participating in an International Study Circle on Women Workers and the Global Food Industry, which ended up recruiting women trade unionists from 11 countries on four continents. WEC produced regular newsletters and updates; acted as a clearing house for developments in grassroots women's education; and also as a conduit to the outside world through requests to its members to speak at conferences, contribute articles and act as consultants.

Despite the dispiriting times, there was no shortage of inspirational achievements. Some wonderful, important, radical, challenging work was being done by WEA women field staff, tutors and branch members, who worked tirelessly, and often thanklessly, to generate funding from any available source. There were too many projects to mention, and it would be invidious to single any one out, but certain highlights stay in the memory: a women's centre in Reading full each day with ethnic minority women; a Young Mums' group and a women's choir in Staffordshire (which performed at a memorable NIACE International Women's Day conference); the Women and Health programme in Kent and Sussex; a group of women from the Dearne Valley, South Yorkshire who came together during the miner's strike and stayed together to get an education and set up a WEA women's branch; women in Rochdale who provided 24-hour round-the-clock support for abused women; a group of Muslim women from Yorkshire who overcame massive cultural and personal obstacles to pursue their learning and become tutors themselves.

Much of this work went unrecorded and unrecognised, but in 1993, three of the six national NIACE Awards for Good Practice in Women's Education went to the WEA. In addition, WEC published reports of the outreach projects funded by the Margaret James Development Fund, and in 1998 a WEC member suggested establishing the Margaret James Award for Good Practice in Women's Education, to be awarded at the WEA's biennial Conference, thus both highlighting the work, and honouring the memory of

Margaret. In 1999, the inaugural prize was fittingly awarded by Veronica McGivney, whose inspirational research and writings had often informed the work and helped argue the case for women's education.

As the century turned, WEC's life and the James bequest were both drawing to an end. The National Women's Education post disappeared as a result of a radical re-organisation in response to the crisis which occurred in the WEA's centenary year, and which resulted in the WEA's incorporation into the educational mainstream.

As we have noted, most of the central support of women's education in the WEA in the 1990s was only made possible by the sum of money bequeathed to the Association by Margaret James. Who was she? What was her interest in women's emancipation? It seemed important to find out more about her so a WEC member set out on her trail, a difficult task from the outset as virtually nothing was known of her. A painstaking, 'white-gloved' search through Annual Reports of the 1930s in the WEA archives at London Guildhall University provided the first clue. She had made her will in 1935, leaving half of her considerable estate (about £19,000 in 1943) to 'The President of the Workers' Educational Association, Professor R.H. Tawney, for the founding of a University Scholarship for the benefit of a working class woman, preferably a member of a Workers' Educational Association class' (for a fuller account of Annie's report see Munby, 2003, pp. 70–72). As we have seen, by the 1990s that sum was worth over £90,000.

Margaret was born in 1901, the daughter of a Nottingham Master Draper and his wife, also Margaret (nee Hastings). She attended Nottingham Girls High School, and went on to Girton College, Cambridge. Subsequently she became a PhD student at the London School of Economics in the 1920s, working under Professor R.H. Tawney, who was President of the WEA for 17 years, and has been hailed as 'the patron saint of adult education' (Elsey, 1987). Perhaps it was a combination of her own educational journey, unusual for a women of her time, and the influence of R.H. Tawney, that persuaded her to leave her money as she did.

Margaret James became a distinguished scholar, a professional historian, especially of the English Civil War, about which she published a book in 1930 (James, 1930). She was highly regarded by, among others, the great radical historian Christopher Hill, and was mentioned in his 2003 obituary (Kettle, 2003). As late as 1974, thirty years after her death, he dedicated a book to her (and another historian) in the following terms:

Both died tragically and prematurely, but not before they had opened up new areas of research which historians are still exploring. An awareness of the pioneering significance of their work was forced on me again and again whilst writing this book. (Hill, 1974)

Margaret died in 1943. According to her death certificate, she committed suicide by throwing herself from an upstairs window 'while the balance of her mind was disturbed', a tragedy the cause of which is yet unknown.

By the WEA centenary year of 2003 women's education as a visible priority area in the WEA had ended. This is not to say it no longer takes place (WEC's influence still lingers), but it is currently neither identified nor resourced as such. It would be understandable at this point in the story to conclude that the current ideological climate, coupled with the elision of the equality debate from the intractable issues of class and gender into the softer and politically expedient 'diversity and difference' agenda, have irrevocably reduced the creative potential of our education system – of its thinking, practice, imagination and spirit. Perhaps this is the case, and the 'gift' that was women's education has been finally rendered lifeless by the clasp of 'their' iron fist.

However, one of the final, and most enduring, gifts that Margaret James bequeathed us was the funding to support a research and oral history project, co-ordinated by a WEA staff member who was also a feminist historian. Hundreds of stories were collected, and a representative range of these were included in a publication, *Raising Our Voices: 100 Years of Women in the WEA* (Munby, 2003).

It is a unique document, bearing witness to the durability of women's determination to educate themselves in ways which speak to them and for them. It shows how the energy of movements waxes and wanes, how cycles come and go, and ways of expressing desire for change and liberation evolve. If history really does repeat itself, *Raising Our Voices* gives cause for optimism. It also provides eloquent testimony to the incalculable contribution women have made, as volunteers, staff, part-time tutors and students, to the WEA over its first century. It was launched at a reception at the Women's Library in London in 2003 with a speech from Sally Alexander, one of the first WEA women's studies tutors. Fittingly, among the many other luminaries present to share the celebration with us was none other than Frances and Albert Mansbridges' granddaughter.

So what are the contributions of women's education in the WEA to the wider learning community? We would suggest that one is to help keep alive the democratic tradition of education. By that we mean education that is primarily concerned with critical reflection, personal development and unending inquiry into the various forms of meaning. It has very little, if anything, to do with getting qualifications, training for our economic role or demonstrating that we have achieved our learning outcomes. That is arguably the task of other institutions, but not of women's education.

The other responsibility is to provide a useful and concrete example to those movements, social or political or educational, transient or centuries old, which find themselves existing on the margins or being pushed back to the borders after a short period of gains. We want the story of women's education in the WEA to speak to those educational, social, political movements which seem caught up in a cycle of ever-repeating marginalisation and powerlessness. We want, in short, to say something about being perceived as dinosaurs and remark on the little observed fact that dinosaurs left large and permanent footprints, prints big enough to track, walk in, and provide a trajectory onwards.

References

Aird, E. (1982) *A Gift in our Hand*, WEA Northern District

Alfred, D. (1987) 'Albert Mansbridge' in Jarvis, P (ed) *Twentieth Century Thinkers in Adult Education*, London: Croom Helm, p. 20

Barr, J. (1984) 'The ways forward. Making our future: Change in women's education', Report of WEA Conference, Durham

Benn, R. (1996) 'Women and Adult Education' in Fieldhouse, R. *et al* (eds) *A History of Modern British Adult Education*, Leicester: NIACE, p. 376

Carnegie UK Trustees (1928) 'The Tutor in Adult Education: An enquiry into the problems of supply and training', in *Report of a Joint Committee appointed by the British Institute of Adult Education and the Tutors Association*, Dunfermline: Carnegie United Kingdom Trustees

Elsey, B. (1987) 'R. H. Tawney – Patron Saint of Adult Education', in Jarvis, P. (ed) *Twentieth Century Thinkers in Adult Education*, London: Croom Helm, pp. 62–76

Hill, C. (1974) 'Dedication', in *Change and Continuity in 17th Century England*, London

Hinder, R. (unknown) *Early days in the WEA 1910–1916*, Unpublished Reading Branch Archives

Hunter, P. and Clarke, M. (2003) *Women and the WEA in Reading: The First 25 Years* (unpublished)

James, M. (1930) *Social Problems and Policy in the Puritan Revolution*, London: Routledge

Kettle, M. (2003) 'Obituary of Christopher Hill', *Guardian*, 26 February 2003

Marsh, G. (2000) *Mansbridge: A Life*, London: WEA

Munby, Z. (2003) 'Alice Wall 1884–1974', in Munby (ed) *Raising Our Voices – 100 years of Women in the WEA*, London: WEA

Scarlett, C. and Winner, A. (1995) 'Quality issues in informal women's education in the voluntary sector', *Adults Learning*, 7(3): 60–62

WEA (1928) *Opportunities for Women in the WEA*, housed in WEA Archive: London Metropolitan University

WEA (1944) *Berks, Bucks & Oxon District Annual Report (1943/4)*, WEA

WEA (1989) *Women's Education Past, Present and Future – A WEA Policy Statement*, London: WEA

Note

[1] The title comes from the reprinted 1912 *Women in the Workers' Educational Association* which was republished, with an accompanying essay by Eileen Aird, as *A Gift in our Hand* in 1982 by the Northern District WEA.

Note from authors

This contribution represents a fragment of the tapestry which is women's education in the WEA during the past one hundred years. We cannot speak for the thousands of women whose lives have been transformed as students, tutors, organisers, researchers, by their experience of women's education in the Association. All we can do is offer our very partial account, honed from a combined total of over fifty years' experience in the WEA. Perhaps one day the story will be written in full. This piece is dedicated to, and acknowledges the work of, those throughout the WEA who are still working for the genuine empowerment of women.

Chapter 6

Social class and widening participation

Richard Taylor

All governments in Britain over the last fifty years or so have emphasised the importance of achieving equality of opportunity in education, and in the social policy context generally. Similar aspirations have been voiced with greater or lesser enthusiasm, by most governments in most developed societies. This emphasis has been particularly apparent in the New Labour government since 1997. And yet, inequality remains stubbornly persistent. Inequality, in relative terms, has actually increased under New Labour; and in education in particular there are clearly differential opportunities at both school and post-compulsory levels.

Everyone, or almost everyone, agrees that the consequences of such inequality are negative in a variety of respects. But the explanation for persisting inequality, and thus the strategies to be adopted to counter it, are contested.

In the past, almost all institutions and social scientists agree that social class has been fundamental to all Western societies' structures and ideologies since the late eighteenth or early nineteenth centuries. Social *inequality* has, of course, a much longer lineage: social class is very much a modernist construct, and indeed material reality.

Social class can be defined as 'a social group, conceived and located in a hierarchical order of unequal such groups, the identity and membership of which is primarily determined by "economic" considerations, such as occupation, income and wealth' (Milner, 1999, p. 1). Two characteristics of social class in modern societies stand out: mutability and mobility. A rather different, but crucial, aspect of class in modern society is the prevalence of 'class consciousness'.

Given that social class has been such a key element of modern societies – and forms the bedrock of much of the academic study of sociology and politics, as in the work of Marx and Weber in particular – how can it be that social class has become currently so 'unfashionable'? That this is the case can hardly be doubted: Stefan Collini, for example, noted as long ago as 1994 in the *Times Literary Supplement* that of the 'quartet of race, class, gender and sexual orientation, there is no doubt that class has been the least fashionable . . .' (Collini, 1994, p. 3). If anything, concepts of class have become even less 'fashionable' since then. In the case of our own specific concerns, it is true that New Labour has belatedly acknowledged that social class is the key element in the widening participation policy agenda. However, the terminology used is almost always constructed so as to avoid the term itself: thus 'social exclusion/inclusion', 'socio-economic disadvantage', and so on. This reflects clearly the reluctance of New Labour to embrace any element of socialist analysis and to recast social and political reality within its own ideological framework. In the specific context of widening participation, it is within this particular ideological reformulation that policy has to be analysed.

So why is it that social class has been downgraded, if not wholly discarded in both intellectual and political circles? The most obvious explanation is that class has ceased to be of central empirical significance in modern societies. This position has been articulated, with greater or lesser force and often hedged around with caveats, by a wide range of prominent analysts and thinkers (Bauman, 1992; Lyotard, 1984; Giddens, 1994). Such disavowals of the centrality of social class are without foundation. In 1988, Marshall *et al*, in a large-scale survey, found that in Britain 90 per cent were able to place themselves as working class or middle class, and 73 per cent believed that class was 'an inevitable feature of modern society' (Marshall *et al*, 1999, p. 247). In a later work, in 1997, Marshall found that there had been virtually no change in social mobility in Britain since 1945 (Marshall, 1997). There has been a 'failure of post-war social policy in almost all industrial nations to achieve [the] declared aims of diminishing class differentials in distributive outcomes' (Marshall, 1997, p. 13). Wright came to similar conclusions in 1997 in a detailed survey of class in the USA, Japan and Sweden. As far as the British New Labour governments since 1997 are concerned, it is now well established that, despite some relatively modest improvements for some of the very poorest groups in the UK, differential inequalities have increased significantly (Toynbee and Walker, 2001). In terms of widening participation, to a discussion of which the second half of this paper is devoted, there is again no question that social class is the key problem internationally, as well as in the specifically British context. David Watson, for example, a noted educationalist, puts it unequivocally: '[t]he key determinant is good, old-fashioned socio-economic circumstances; in short it is class' (Watson, 2005, p. 37).

Postmodernist, thoreticist critiques, which decentre class in contemporary frameworks are thus, in John Goldthorpe's phrase, distinctive in being 'data-free'. How is this widespread perception to be explained? And what is the correct analysis of class in contemporary late capitalist societies – particularly, for the purposes of this paper, Britain?

A prominent exponent of New Labour ideology, and a noted sociologist, Anthony Giddens is among those who have written of the demise of socialism. Not only has the Soviet Union collapsed, but also what he describes as 'welfare socialism' has proved to be unattainable. '[W]ith this realisation, the history of socialism as the *avant-garde* of political theory comes to a close' (Giddens, 1994, p. 69). Giddens had originally been a radical socialist sociologist. Even more dramatically, two of the leading postmodernist theorists, Baudrillard and Lyotard, were both originally members of the small, extreme anarcho-syndicalist group 'Socialisme ou Barbarie', and their *volte face* was thus even more total[1].

The explanation is more likely to be, as so often, political and ideological, rather than the result of theoretical advances, let alone solid evidence. The collapse of communism, the discrediting of Marxism, Leninism and indeed of Western Eurocommision and its variants, and the retreats of social democracy in almost all Western societies, have been accompanied by a strongly revisionist move in intellectual and academic theorisation and analysis. (There are though major exceptions to this generalisation in other parts of the world, not least South America, the Indian subcontinent and, of course, China.)

This has been though a purely ideological and political shift: there is no change in the realities of the inequalities experienced in the capitalist system. The internal crisis of the Left, and the vacuum created by the closure of opportunities for socialist restructuring, are certainly important – and material political facts in their own right. But there is clearly no substantive case for the view that social class and inequality have ceased to be relevant factors in social and political analysis. It is the historical, ideological and emotive connections between social class and socialist theorisation that have been the 'problem'. The 'decentring' of class has thus been the result of the disillusionment and reaction of large numbers of intellectuals and political activists, in the wake of the political reverses that socialism, in all its forms, has certainly undergone in the last twenty-five years or so.

All this is not to claim in any way that class structures have not changed: obviously they have, and they are now probably more volatile and complex than at any previous period. Still less is it to claim that Marxist analysis, especially Marx's own, are wholly accurate. Nevertheless, it is important to note at the outset of this part of the argument that many of Marx's ideas and perceptions about class *have* been borne out by historical developments in the twentieth and early twenty-first centuries. Capital has become increasingly concentrated, thus fuelling increasing inequalities; the numbers of those in the economy who are employees have risen (though the marked predominance in western societies of 'white-collar' workers was not foreseen); correspondingly, the numbers of self-employed declined substantially from the late nineteenth to the late twentieth century (though this trend has been reversed to an extent in more recent years); and there is considerable evidence for a long-run decline in profitability. At a more general level, few can deny that the irrational, anarchic and exploitative nature of international capitalism, and its barbaric consequences, have intensified in the global age (Callinicos, 1989; Pilger, 1998).

On the other hand, at least since 1945, Western societies have not been 'pauperised', as Marx had predicted; nor, generally, have Western economies been prone to crises of over-production since the post-1945 Keynesian revolution in economics; and, whether or not because of 'false consciousness' (the Marxist catch-all, when all else fails), there has been, generally, no polarisation of social classes, and thus no widespread class conflict.

As far as Britain is concerned, John Westergaard's typology, first articulated in the mid-1970s, but reconfirmed by subsequent analyses and discussion in the years since, offers the most appropriate delineation of actually existing class structures, albeit with one major omission (Westergaard and Resler, 1975; Westergaard, 1995; Westergaard, 1996). He identifies three broad classes in contemporary Britain: a small layer of directors, managers, established high-status professionals and officers; an intermediate group of those who sell their labour at a relatively high premium (lower level managers, technicians, supervisors, etc.); and the broad mass of ordinary wage earners, including an increasing proportion of 'white-collar' workers. The glaring omission from this typology is the deep-rooted, persisting wealth of the 'old order' and its culture. In his definitive analysis of almost fifty years ago (Anderson, 1961), Perry Anderson identified this phenomenon of the continuity and persistence of the landed aristocracy's power base, economically and culturally, as the prime cause of Britain's partially achieved – if not aborted – bourgeois revolution. The concomitant of this, as Anderson argued convincingly (despite Edward Thompson's eloquent, romantic and impassioned rebuttal (Thompson, 1965)) was the evolution of a generally supine and incorporated Labour movement in the nineteenth and twentieth centuries. The accuracy of this analysis is portrayed in all its awfulness in New Labour.

Empirically, there are several other fairly new and certainly important factors to be noted, all of them linked: there has been a marked feminisation of the workforce over the last forty years, but especially since the mid-1980s. (In Britain, for example, there were in 2005 12.5 million women in employment, compared with 9.1 million in 1975, and pay differentials and the status of jobs held between men and women, though still marked, have decreased (Equal Opportunities Commission, 2005).) Flexible and part-time working have become far more common, as has occupational mobility. And there has been a marked reduction in trade union membership following the Thatcherite dominance in the 1980s (though this has stabilised and is increasing, slowly, in the early twenty-first century). In Westergaard's view, by the mid-1990s, class structures had hardened: '. . . it (class) has been re-declared dead . . . at a time . . . when its economic configuration has become even sharper' (Westergaard, 1995, pp. 113–114).

One of the few themes of post-modernism that can claim validity is the contention that late capitalist society is characterised by volatility, complexity and flexibility. In relation to social class, Frederic Jameson takes up the point and argues convincingly that commodification of hitherto uncommodified areas is significant. Further, because both theorists and political ideologues are determined to sideline class as an important facet of contemporary society, 'reification . . . is very functional indeed' (Jameson, 1991, p. 315). This process is now well-advanced and it is therefore reasonable to surmise that, given the incompatibility of material reality and ideological perception, political class consciousness is on hold until the new global economy has produced a more stable and explicit class formation, or series of formations. For the short-term, it is generally to social movements, rather than the established political parties, that radicals should therefore look for indications of emergent new structures.

Widening participation policy

All this, however, seems rather far-removed from the pragmatic grind of New Labour's widening participation policy. There is no doubt that widening participation has been a key policy objective for New Labour, across the whole of the post-compulsory sector. (However, at the time of writing – early 2006 – it is clear that widening participation has ceased to be a major driving force in policy. This is probably the result of 'concept fatigue' plus a more substantive move even further to the right in New Labour ideology.) The low level of participation in education and training, post-school, is a notorious characteristic of British society, and, like the class-stratified school system, this reflects the overall inequality of British society. One of the most creditable aspects of New Labour's education policy since 1997 has been the advocacy of widening participation, and this policy rhetoric has been backed up, to an extent, by directed funding.

In the early years of the 1997 Labour Government, there was a real excitement and transformative spirit in policy discussions (Taylor, 2005). The flurry of reports and commissions – Dearing, Kennedy and Fryer – all had widening participation and lifelong learning at their core. However, as I have argued elsewhere (Taylor, 2005), this mood of optimism and dynamism was relatively short-lived. Nevertheless, the Prime Minister's commitment to the 50 per cent participation rate in higher education by 2010 was (and to an extent remains) a high profile policy commitment. Less prominent, but equally ambitious, are the Government's targets for basic education, and for levels 2 and 3 (NVQ) attainment.

However, New Labour's definition, purpose and overall ideology of widening participation are very different indeed from those of the Labour movement in any previous period. R.H. Tawney is a good and prominent example of traditional left of centre Labour thinking[2]. Tawney saw widening participation as both a moral imperative and a fundamental aspect of emancipation and empowerment of the working class. This is neither the language nor the ideology of New Labour. The primary purpose of widening participation for New Labour is to increase economic efficiency in an increasingly complex and knowledge-orientated economy. The rationale is thus primarily utilitarian, and the education and training envisaged largely instrumental. Despite all the evidence to the contrary, (Coffield, 1998, 1999) policy is based upon 'human capital' arguments, with increasing emphases upon the 'lower levels' for widening participation students in the two related contexts of further and higher education. For example, in higher education there is a strong focus, mirrored in funding structures, upon foundation degree developments, which are explicitly at 'sub-degree' level and strongly vocational, both substantively and in their ethos.

Thus, in its essentials, it could be argued that what drives New Labour's widening participation policy is the perception that a higher, but still intermediate, skills level is required for the labour market in order to ensure Britain's future economic competitiveness. There is little other than rhetoric in the Government's commitment to education for its own, liberating, sake; still less is there any conception of social purpose, seeing widening participation, as Tawney did, as a key element in socialist emancipation. David Blunkett's Preface to *The Learning Age* – a passionate avocation of the liberal education idea, and the emancipatory power of educational involvement – seems a long time ago (Blunkett, 1997).

Another issue with widening participation policy can be represented by the question 'Access to what?' There are two negative aspects to this. First, the large majority of widening participation involvement in higher education – and this is mirrored in other post-compulsory sectors – is in both vocational and 'non-standard' areas. There has been little incursion into the heartlands of the system. The norm, in higher education, remains as strongly as ever the three-year full-time honours degree in traditional academic subjects. Widening participation students and their often non-standard mode and subject focus are thus still regarded as marginal, albeit usually implicitly. It is of course the case that widening participation has become a sector-wide concern; and there is no doubt that the pre-1992 universities are taking the issue reasonably seriously. However, and perhaps understandably, this boils down to providing generous bursaries and extending existing schools' compact schemes to attract a small number of highly able students from educationally (and socially) deprived backgrounds.

Secondly, and linked to this, a clear pattern has emerged that 'widening participation' students in higher education are confined largely to post-1992, low status institutions. (Such terminology is not to make a value judgement, merely to be frank about the factual and cultural position in our very stratified educational system.) This is often linked to relatively low status occupations, following the educational involvement. There are, of course, exceptions, but this is very much the rule, as numerous studies have shown, and is wholly predictable (see HEFCE policy documents on Widening Participation, 1997 to 2005; Taylor, Barr and Steele, 2002).

From a lifelong learning viewpoint, one of the most depressing aspects of New Labour's policy in this area is its persistent and increasing marginalisation of adult learners. The whole concentration, both in the FE sector, as illustrated by LSC policies, and in the HE sector, has been upon younger learners, particularly the 17–21 age cohort. Even from a human capital perspective, this makes no sense, given the demographic projections for a shrinking workforce and an ageing population, not only in Britain but in almost all developed societies. The emphases, however, are undeniable: the latest examples in Britain being, first, the shambles over part-time and adult learning in the 2005 Higher Education Act; and, second, the drastic cutbacks in 2005 and 2006 that have seen many HE and FE programmes, especially those in liberal studies and so-called recreational education, very severely reduced. Both these categories of learners have substantial numbers of disadvantaged, working-class people of all ages, coming to education and learning late because of poor schooling and the lack of a supportive social and cultural environment.

Another central dimension of New Labour's ideology is relevant to this policy formulation: the rejection of all collective ideology, which had characterised 'Old Labour', and indeed all socialist ideology. In its place, New Labour has adopted a wholly individualistic frame of reference. It is the individual in the market place, the learner as customer, that defines the widening participation context for Labour policy. Virtually all initiatives in policy in this area are aimed at, and judged by, the success of *individuals* rather than communities, or other collective groups. Thus education is a commodity to be invested in on criteria similar to any other capital investment. There is precious little acknowledgement here of liberal education, of education and learning as a central aspect of a civilised and democratic society. New Labour is not only a long way from any concept of socialism, it is also in contradiction with the liberal educational philosophy of Cardinal Newman and the emancipatory, democratic educational philosophy of R.H. Tawney.

What then should we, as enthusiasts for lifelong learning, be advocating, realistically, over the next few years? And how can this address the persistent class inequality that is at the heart of Britain's capitalist system? I have argued throughout this paper that the fundamental problems are ideological and political. Solutions, or at least some improvement in the current position, thus require ideological and political approaches. Blairite conceptions of widening participation must be challenged and exposed as superficial and ideologically-driven falsehoods. These perspectives derive from the rhetoric of market ideology.

The claims of New Labour's position are little short of bizarre. To begin with, as demonstrated here, there is overwhelming evidence that social class, deriving from persisting inequalities and the inherent, historic structure of capitalism, continues to dominate social structures in late capitalist societies. Secondly, the topsy-turvy world that market ideologues have tried to create is patently absurd. As Thomas Frank has argued, market ideology in the 1990s became equated with democratisation.

> Since it was markets that expressed the will of the people, virtually any criticism of business could be described as an act of elitism arising out of despicable contempt for the common man . . . the elitists were the people on the other side of the equation: the trade unionists and Keynesians who believed that society could be organised in any way other than the market way. (Frank, 2001)

Or, as the *Wall Street Journal* put it during the American presidential election campaign in 2001, 'Mr Bush should tell Americans [that] when my opponent attacks big corporations, he is attacking you and me' (Taranto, 2000). Given the demonstrably rapacious nature of global capital, and the systematic suppression, or attempted suppression, by the governments of capitalist states and multi-national companies, especially the United States of America and its big corporations (Pinter, 2005; Pilger, 1998; Hutton, 2002), this is a truly 'Orwellian' claim. This is a supreme example of the attempted engendering of false consciousness on a grand scale.

The development of more radical perspectives on widening participation take place in this context. Devising the *tactics* to confront New Labour's position is always complex, often contentious: but there can be no doubt about the *strategy*. In terms of specific issues, I would highlight two. The first is the danger that widening participation will be confined to the lower status institutions and sectors. Thus, in higher education, there is an ostensibly convincing argument that widening participation should be confined to the post-1992 institutions. Such HEIs, it can be argued, have the 'mission', the expertise and the cultural ethos for such cohorts. Moreover, from the managerial perspective in such HEIs, it can be argued that the post-1992 universities should have the 'widening participation resources', almost as a *quid pro quo*, for the older universities taking virtually all of the 'quality of research' (QR) resources via the Research Assessment Exercise. However, given the hierarchical and status structure of the British system, such a 'ghettoising' of widening participation will merely exacerbate existing inequalities and confirm systemic class structures. It is thus essential for lifelong learning to permeate all parts of the sector, and our policy formulation should centre on this principle.

Secondly, and more fundamentally, there is a danger that widening participation will become wholly concerned with process and structure: that is, how do we ensure that more people (of all ages) from disadvantaged social, economic and educational backgrounds can gain access to post-compulsory education and training. Important though this is, and not easy to achieve, as experience has shown, it leaves aside the *purpose* of widening participation – what is it *for*? In the ostensibly 'apolitical' climate of the times, this may be taken as self-evident: it is entirely to enable individuals, within a meritocratic framework, to progress as far as their talents, interests and competence allow – and thereby to enable them to gain material benefit in due course. But it does matter what learners learn; it is important that liberal and critical educational philosophies are articulated; and that the long-established patterns of incorporation which have been so important in the history of the Labour movement in Britain and elsewhere, are avoided.

All post-compulsory education and training should embody both democratic and discursive models of learning, and instil habits of sceptical, critical analysis where all questions are open questions and where minority and dissident perspectives are given particular prominence. Intellectual rigour, critical expertise and the democratic spirit should be the hallmarks of the widening participation learning experience – not the dreary mantra of the often instrumental, unthinking 'skills training' perspective so favoured by human capital advocates.

Widening participation is, or should be, part of an emancipatory social movement, rather than merely a 'policy orientation'. Such a concept is a long way from current New Labour politics. It is our task to instil this counter-ideology into the prevailing common sense.

References

Anderson, Perry (1961) 'Origins of the present crisis', first published in *New Left Review*, reprinted in Tom Nairn and Perry Anderson (eds), *Towards Socialism*, London: Fontana and New Left Books

Bauman, Z. (1992) *Intimations of Postmodernity*, London: Routledge

Blunkett, D. (1997) 'Foreword', in DfES, *The Learning Age*, London: HMSO

Callinicos, A. (1989) *Against Postmodernism: A Marxist Critique*, Cambridge: Polity Press

Coffield, F. (1998) 'Breaking the consensus: lifelong learning, as social control', Inaugural lecture, University of Newcastle, 2 February 1998

Coffield, F. (1999) *Why is the Beer Always Stronger up North? Studies of Lifelong Learning in Europe*, London: Polity Press

Collini, S. (1994) *Times Literary Supplement*, 27 May 1994

Equal Opportunities Commission (2005) Equal Opportunities Commission Report, EOC

Frank, T. (2001) *The Guardian*, 6 January 2001

Giddens, A. (1994) *Beyond Left and Right: The Future of Radical Politics*, Cambridge: Polity Press

HEFCE (1997–2005) Policy documents on Widening Participation, Bristol: HEFCE

Hutton, W. (2002) *The World We're In*, London: Little Brown

Jameson, F. (1991) *Postmodernism, or, The Cultural Logic of Late Capitalism*, London: Verso

Lyotard, J-F. (1984) *The Postmodern Condition: A Report on Knowledge* (translated by G. Bennington and B Massumi), Minneapolis: University of Minnesota Press

Marshall, G. A., Newby, H., Rose, D. and Vogler, C (1999) *Social Class in Modern Britain*, London: Hutchinson

Marshall, G. (1997) *Repositioning Class: Social Inequality in Industrial Societies*, London: Sage

Milner, A. (1999) *Class*, London: Sage

Pilger, J. (1998) *Hidden Agendas*, London: Vintage

Pinter, H. (2005) Acceptance speech on the award of the Nobel Prize for Literature in 2005. Reprinted in *The Guardian*, 9 December 2005

Steele, T. and Taylor, R. (forthcoming 2006) 'R.H. Tawney and the Universities', *History of Education*

Taranto, J. (2000) 'Why class warfare may work this year', *The Wall Street Journal*, Thursday, August 24

Taylor, R. (1983) *The British Nuclear Disarmament Movement of 1958–1965 and its Legacy to the Left*, PhD thesis, University of Leeds, Leeds

Taylor, R. (1988) *Against the Bomb: The British Nuclear Disarmament Movement of 1958 to 1965*, Oxford: Oxford University Press

Taylor, R. (2005) 'Lifelong learning policy and the Labour Governments, 1997–2004', *Oxford Review of Education* (Special edition on the Labour Governments of 1997–2004 and Education Policy), 31(1): 101–118

Taylor, R., Barr, J. and Steele, T. (2002) *For a Radical Higher Education: After Postmodernism*, Buckingham: SRHE and Open University Press

Thompson, E. (1965) 'The peculiarities of the English', first published in *New Left Review*, reprinted in R Miliband and J Saville (eds), *The Socialist Register 1965*, London: Merlin Press

Toynbee, P. and Walker, D. (2001) *Did Things Get Better? An Audit of Labour's Successes and Failures*, London: Penguin

Watson, D. (2005) 'Overview: telling the truth about widening participation' in Geoff Layer (ed), *Closing the Equity Gap, the Impact of Widening Participation Strategies in the UK and USA*, Leicester: NIACE, p. 37.

Westergaard, J. (1979) 'Class in Britain since 1979: facts, theories and ideologies' in D. J. Lee and B. S. Turner (eds) *Conflicts about Class: Debating Inequality in Late Industrialism*, London: Longman

Westergaard, J. (1995) *Who Gets What? The Hardening of Class Inequality in the Late Twentieth Century*, Cambridge: Polity Press

Westergaard, J. and Resler, H. (1975) *Class in a Capitalist Society: A Study of Contemporary Britain*, London: Heinemann

Notes

[1] In Britain, 'Socialisme ou Barbarie' and its ideology was represented in the organisation 'Solidarity for Workers' Power'. This group had a significant influence on the libertarian left, especially in the early nuclear disarmament movement in Britain. For a discussion of its ideology and its influences in the Committee of 100, see Taylor, 1983, 1988.

[2] For a detailed analysis of Tawney's philosophy and his interest and influence upon Labour's educational policy formulation, over a long period, see Steele and Taylor (forthcoming 2006) 'R. H. Tawney and the universities', *History of Education*.

Chapter 7

The 'baby bulge' generation comes to retirement

Stephen McNair

Through the 1970s and 1980s adult educators lobbied, often with little apparent effect, for 'lifelong learning' or variants on the idea. In the last fifteen years we have, at last, got what we said we wanted, and found ourselves facing the hard choices which go with being taken seriously. Which priority groups are most important? What kind of evidence for impact is valid? How should we balance the role of the state, employer and the individual in paying for education and training? Do we need different approaches to learning itself?

One issue which might be expected to change thinking about learning is demography, from two directions: the steady decline in fertility rates in Europe and worldwide, and the dramatic extension of lifespan. The former creates potential economic problems about shortage of labour, currently being met in the UK by an influx of skilled and unskilled labour from the new accession states of the EU and beyond. However, this may well prove only a temporary solution, since in the medium term, those countries themselves face similar demographic patterns. The latter raises more fundamental questions about the distribution of activity across the lifespan, about the boundaries between paid and unpaid work and other activity. Our understanding of it is also being challenged by the arrival in their fifties of the 'bulge generation', who were born immediately after the Second World War, and who have transformed each stage of life as they arrived in it. This is a generation who have, at every stage of the lifecourse, challenged the assumptions of their parents' generation. It would be surprising if they did not want to change our understanding of 'retirement' as well.

Demographic change has altered the nature of the 'normal' lifecourse in the last 50 years. Once the norm was to spend 16–18 years preparing for a working life, 40 or more years working full time (paid or domestic), followed by a short period of 'retirement' as a brief holiday between full-time work and terminal illness. Now young people enter the labour market later, people are more likely to take career breaks, and, until recently, have been retiring earlier. Although the latter trend has halted, current patterns suggest that we are in sight of 'retirement' as 30 years of healthy life, and every decade sees two more years added to average life expectancy. What are we preparing for? What gives life meaning and structure for people whose whole lives have been organised around paid work?

This chapter seeks to explore some of these issues, in the light of recent research into working in later life. It suggests that demographic change sheds a new light on the relationship between work and life, and the learning needs associated with both.

Demography, work and learning in later life

In the last few years falling birthrates and rising life expectancy have made the extension of working life a growing focus of public policy. As the Pensions Commission report pointed out (Pensions Commission, 2004), there are only three options for future policy: pensioners get poorer, everyone saves more for their retirement, or most people will have to work longer. Apart from the moral issue, the first is politically difficult, because older people are more likely to vote, and the second is fine in principle but too late for today's expanding retired population. This leaves the third as the least unappealing, especially since, even if we were to raise average retirement ages by three or four years, most people would still have a longer healthy retirement than the average for the previous generation. Furthermore, although the media have traditionally enjoyed scare stories about government's plans to make people 'work until you drop', the evidence is that, far from being afraid of working longer, most older people are very attached to work: since 1998 the number of people in work after the age of 50 has risen by a million, and the number of people working after State Pension Age has risen by 35 per cent.

However, there are significant barriers to a real extension of working life, of which probably the most powerful has been described as 'the last great unfair discrimination': discrimination on grounds of age. Although age affects us all, public attitudes to ageing workers are still where attitudes to gender were in the early 1960s. Many people are prepared to say things about older people which they would recognise as entirely unacceptable about gender or disability, and many older people themselves accept that they are less competent, less employable and less deserving than their younger peers. Many myths, about low commitment to work, inability to learn and physical incapacity, have been demonstrated to be unfounded, yet they persist in the minds of employers and employees, and although employers rarely report overt discrimination in surveys, qualitative evidence of individuals' experience, and studies which submit paired job applications with different ages, show that it operates on a systematic and widespread basis (reference and date).

The result of this, and other factors is that the labour market, which has become much more flexible generally since the 1970s, remains very rigid for people in later life. After the age of 50, and especially after 55, it is more difficult to get a new job, to get promotion or change role. Although many people would like to stay in work longer, but on a part-time basis, this remains relatively rare, and many older workers fear the risk of appearing uncommitted to the job or firm by seeking downsizing or job change. Others, rightly afraid of being unable to re-enter the workplace once out, settle for sticking in the same job for longer than is good for them, their firms or the economy, thus reinforcing some of the negative stereotypes of older workers which are a major factor in age discrimination.

As a result, after the mid-fifties the workforce is increasingly dominated by three groups: people sticking in their existing jobs rather than risking a move; people with inadequate savings; and people in fields where labour shortages are most severe. After State Pension Age, the pattern changes, and the labour market loses its middle tiers, with those who stay concentrated in three groups: people running their own small businesses; self-employed professionals; and a large group of people in predominantly low-status manual occupations.

However, there is evidence that the barriers can be overcome in areas where labour shortages are severe. In parts of the South East, which have had nearly full employment for some years, and where housing shortages and overloaded transport systems make increased immigration or commuting impractical, labour problems have resulted in the highest 50+ labour market participation rates in Europe (reference, date) (apart from Scandinavia, where working later has always been the norm). The same effect can be seen in some sectors, with some large retailers employing relatively large numbers of older people, in response to general labour shortages, while parts of the health and social care sector retain skilled staff after normal retirement age because of a general shortage of recruits, and the high costs of training new entrants.

Studying the older workforce

In 2003 the South East of England Development Agency commissioned the Centre for Research into the Older Workforce (CROW) to undertake a study of the behaviour of the older labour market, to inform regional economic and training policy. The result has been three interlocking studies. The first was a large-scale quantitative investigation of job change across the workforce, carried out through the Office of National Statistics' monthly national Omnibus survey (5400 respondents of all ages). This aimed to explore how far patterns of job mobility vary with age, and provide a framework for the subsequent work. The second study took 400 of these people in their fifties and sixties, and explored their attitudes to work and retirement, and to public policy on these issues through a postal questionnaire. The third stage consisted of qualitative interviews with 38 people drawn from the second group, exploring in much more detail their individual experiences of work, and especially the influence of education and training on their lives. The use of three interlocking samples enabled each study to illuminate the others, and the final result is an unusually rich body of qualitative data about attitudes and experience, backed up by quantitative evidence about a large and representative population sample.

Do older people like work?

The first, and most striking finding from all three strands of the study is how strongly people like work. In the omnibus survey four out of five of those still in employment after the age of 50 said that they would consider working 'after retirement', provided that it could be flexible. To test how strong this view was, the issue was probed in more detail in the postal survey. There, when offered a range of statements about reasons for liking and disliking work, over 75 per cent of all working people gave positive answers. Over 80 per cent said that they enjoyed their jobs and working with colleagues; that their jobs suited their personal circumstances; and that they made good use of their skills. Although the scores were lower for 'my employer values my work'; 'my job contributes to society'; and 'my experience is valued', they still represented a clear majority (between 66 and 80 per cent).

Since people tend to respond to such surveys in ways which justify the choices they have already made, one might expect to find more negative views of work among those who have already retired (at whatever age), but the reverse was true. When people in this group were asked the same questions (about their last paid job), their responses on all questions were more positive than the employed group, especially on the questions 'I enjoyed working with my colleagues' and 'my job was enjoyable'. When asked about the decision to retire, three-quarters said that they were happy not to be in paid work, but a majority also said that they now wish that they could have stayed in work but worked flexibly or fewer hours. The most positive attitudes to work were found among those who described themselves as 'retired', but were in part-time paid work of some kind, all of whom gave positive responses to the last two questions.

The postal survey also asked for views on the retirement policy options on which the Government was consulting at the time. Almost all (93 per cent), working and retired, agreed that 'so long as they are fit and capable, people should be able to continue working, whatever their age', and over a quarter even agreed with 'now that most people are living longer, it is reasonable to raise the State Pension Age'. Interestingly, however, despite very positive responses to 'my job makes good use of my skills', 90 per cent of people felt that 'the skills and talents of older people are not being put to best use in Britain'. This suggests an interesting discontinuity between peoples' perceptions of their own situation and that of other people, and perhaps between those in work and those seeking it. The latter is confirmed by evidence from the qualitative survey, where several people in their fifties said that they were personally valued by their employer, but that their employer discriminates against other (sometimes younger) people who were seen as 'too old'.

The three surveys together also give a good picture of what older people like about work, and it is notable how widespread positive attitudes to work were among a sample including a golf club barmaid, a senior manager in the Fire Service, a train cleaner, a senior nurse and a gravedigger. Flexibility and control head the list of things which make work attractive to people, but they also value the social contact with colleagues, the ability to use their skills, a sense of contributing to society, a sense of challenge and the opportunity to learn something new. The opportunity to work flexibly and to fit the job around personal circumstances was important to most, and working locally mattered to many. For most, the field of work itself was important, and in the qualitative interviews several people talked about attachment to the job content, sometimes in terms of an interest they expected to continue to pursue after ceasing paid work. One described the job he is now doing as 'an opportunity to make a job out of my hobby', and another, working as a barmaid in a golf club, talked about her passion for golf. One woman, a train cleaner, talked about pride in doing the job well, and like several others, contrasted her own sense of this with that of younger colleagues, or of part timers, 'with part-time work comes a part-time attitude' (which contrasts interestingly with the demand for part-time work from older people generally).

Respect was clearly an issue for some, with the sense of one's experience being devalued or ignored as a powerful motivator for leaving the workplace. Money, on the other hand, was not a major factor in most of the interviews, and while this may be a traditional reticence to discuss such matters, it matches the evidence from the Joseph Rowntree Foundation's research (reference, date) that money plays a relatively small part in retirement decisions, either because older people are resigned to living on whatever income level they will have or are unable to understand the complexities of retirement finance. Even the interviewee who talked most strongly about financial need, also talked very positively about work in the past and continuing to work in the future

> . . . I won't be able to afford to retire. I wouldn't have enough unless I win the lottery at the weekend. But then again if I win the lottery I think I'll still work because I'd be bored . . . I enjoy my job I must admit. I've enjoyed all my jobs even the grave digging although it's hard work at times. But I enjoy the work.

Taken together these are striking findings: that people like work, that they would like to work longer if they could do so on a part-time basis, and that those who manage to do this are the most likely to be satisfied with their situation.

The life history interviews with individuals in their fifties and sixties provide the richest insights into people's attitudes to work and learning across the lifespan. The most striking evidence is the unpredictability of career paths, and of motivation. Several talked about false starts, often under the influence of parents who wanted them to follow in parental footsteps or to find a 'safer' job than their parents. Some abandoned these routes early, while at least one, looking back on a lifetime of nursing, still felt that she had made the wrong choice. It is evident that such problems will never be solved by better initial career planning: since individuals will take time to identify a sense of purpose and direction for their working and personal lives, and they can and do change direction, one clear message is that concentrating all resources on initial careers advice and guidance is as inappropriate as doing the same for education.

This generation was the first to experience the selective secondary education system of the Butler Education Act, and although the scars remain for those who perceive themselves to have been unfairly treated these do not seem to have permanently affected attitudes to learning. One graphically described the reason for leaving school before his 15th birthday as 'it was kicking out time', and talked about the absence of the 'vocational' education which Butler had promised: 'they occasionally took you out on the garden patch, if that was vocational'. However, he then went to work as a hospital technician, completing some years later a loosely related City & Guilds qualification, and spending most of his career in the hospital's medical physics department, acquiring through experience and observation the skills and knowledge which would now be sought through degree-level qualifications. Eventually he chose to retire because he saw a new managerial culture creating divisions and valuing formal qualifications more highly than his experience. Another began life as a wages clerk, going on to spend years as a professional gardener, and ending up as a care worker, each time undertaking formal training (and acquiring in the process a sophisticated understanding of the workings of qualifications systems).

Despite long, and often successful, working careers, a surprising number of interviewees still lacked confidence in their own abilities. The sense of being an impostor was surprisingly common, and several talked about not being as well qualified as their younger peers, and having 'only' learned by practice on the job. In an extreme case one man's learning career, which included five separate qualifications (including three degrees and a teaching qualification) following what he describes as a disastrous initial career choice, resulting from difficult home circumstances, illustrates the complexities of learning motivation across a lifetime. His story reads as a repeated struggle to convince himself of his own (repeatedly demonstrated) ability.

Despite the anxieties, among the interviewees were several with an evident passion for learning, for themselves and for others, most notably among the three interviewees who worked in the NHS, whose learning culture clearly pervaded their thinking about work itself. Indeed, they were the only people who talked at length, and with real enthusiasm, about their own training, and their role in training colleagues. At the same time, respondents were generally very aware of the pressures on their employers over release for training, noting (without obvious resentment) that they would have liked to train more, but that the demands of the work had to come first. However, two did report having refused training offers from their employers, on the grounds that they were too near retirement to justify the effort and expense.

Intergenerational attitudes were clearly important in how people thought about work in later life, and in the decision to retire. Several talked about taking on formal or informal mentoring roles with younger colleagues, sometimes much better qualified in formal terms. However, attitudes to younger managers and to organisational change were more negative, and a powerful strand of resentment at organisational change, and lack of trust from managers or government was very evident among those in public sector work.

Towards an 'extended lifecourse' model

For most of the twentieth century, the commonly accepted view of working life was of labour market entry after initial education, a 'career' involving a progressive climb (for most people) to a plateau, and ending abruptly in a short period of retirement, ill health and death. Although this pattern is now far from universal, it remains the dominant model in much policy thinking and resource allocation, and it influences the priorities of study in many academic disciplines. The CROW studies suggest that, as the post-war 'bulge' generation reach their fifties, the model no longer matches the aspirations of people. It is also increasingly inappropriate in terms of economic need for skilled and experienced workers in many sectors facing a shrinking workforce.

One might expect this to present an ideal conjunction: people want to work longer, employers need them to stay longer, and government wants them to do so. However, there are a series of underlying challenges. People mistrust government, particularly in relation to long-term commitments over issues like pensions. One CROW informant noted that it was wise to take the offer of early retirement during an organisational restructuring, because the pension offer might not be there in five years time. Many employers have not yet fully recognised the implications of the demographic challenge, believing that somehow their sector or firm will beat the trend and continue to recruit young people, and failing to recognise that the economic and demographic trends together are shifting the balance of power between employer and worker, as labour gets scarcer, and older workers have the opportunity to withdraw from work if it is not offered in attractive forms.

A further problem is that the field is relatively under-researched, and we lack good conceptual and theoretical models to understand it. For the last 60 years the population of 'working age' (i.e. below State Pension Age) was growing almost continuously. As a result, the priorities were to ensure that new entrants to the workforce were well prepared and productive, and that a certain amount of training was available to keep people in mid-career up-to-date, and allow for an element of mobility within the market (like women re-entering, or the unemployed returning). The final years were not seen as important, either because most people wanted to leave at the earliest possible opportunity (and 'early retirement' was generally seen as a benefit, as well as a convenient way of managing organisational change), or, less positively, because people would drop out when they were worn out, or the market no longer needed them. Perhaps, when life expectancy was shorter, and most employment more physically demanding, the former was true. If the latter ever was true, it is clearly no longer so.

However, the historically unprecedented halting of workforce expansion, coupled with continuing economic growth and extending life expectancy, is reversing these trends. Slowly the market is beginning to recognise that it needs people to stay longer, and that many older workers have skills and knowledge which are hard to replace, making retention a more cost-effective strategy than recruitment for many roles. However, older workers are different from their younger peers in that there is, at some stage within sight, the option to stop work altogether. For almost all young people work is a necessity, and an unattractive job can only be traded for another job, which gives the employer a powerful lever to exercise in the labour market. At some point during their fifties, however, most people arrive at a point where they believe they have the option to escape from unattractive work in return for a lower, but perhaps manageable, income in retirement. If employers wish to keep such employees longer, they will have to ensure that work is designed in ways which appeal to the aspirations of employees, and the evidence is that, in sectors or regions where skilled labour is in short supply (the South-East of England, retail and the health service), employer behaviour is already changing. As the CROW evidence indicates, among older people the motivation to work is strong, provided that the work provides a degree of autonomy, flexibility, social engagement and respect.

One consequence of the nature of the 'old' labour market is that the processes of exit, and the nature of work in later life were of little interest to policy-makers or researchers. Sociologists, economists and industrial relations specialists were more interested in the processes of entry to the labour market, in interrupted careers and progression, in discrimination against particular groups, or more recently with issues of work-life balance. Where sociologists and educational gerontologists considered older people, it was in the context of life after employment and old age, and the notion that 'life is more than work' was a powerful driver.

Even for adult educators, who have always known from experience the waste and injustice of a 'front end' model of learning, much of the focus of 'lifelong' policy debates has really been on late entry and mid-life return. After decades of attending to the learning needs of those who change their minds in their twenties; of women returners in their thirties; and of those facing redundancy and unemployment in their forties, it is perhaps time to look harder at how extended working life affects learning needs for people in their fifties and sixties, not in terms of 'preparing for retirement', but of more complex work and life transitions. What are the implications of extra decades of healthy active life, for work, for social relationships and for the meaning of life?

During the last twenty years, the work of Veronica McGivney for NIACE has made a huge contribution to increasing our understanding of what motivates adults to learn, and what prevents them from doing so. Government policy has changed in relation to adults with literacy and numeracy problems, to women returners, and to mature entrants to higher education, to mention only three groups. One of the real challenges of the next decade will be to understand how to reconfigure work and learning, and the relationships between them, in a population and workforce with a greater age span, and a greater diversity of working and learning roles and relationships. At each stage of the lifecourse, the post-war 'bulge' generation of which Veronica has been a part has changed our understanding of what is possible for human beings. It is not surprising that this is now exerting pressure on our understanding of retirement and later life. There is much to do to overcome discrimination, to open up opportunities, and to enable older workers to experience the same kinds of challenges that this generation brought to the earlier stages of their lives.

References

Pensions Commission (2004) *Pensions Challenges and Choices: The First Report of the Pensions Commission*, London: TSO

Robertson, I., Warr, P., Butcher, V., Callinan, M. and Bradzil, P. (2003) *Older People's Experience of Paid Employment: Participation and Quality of Life*, Sheffield: Growing Older Programme

Notes

[1] The latter finding is supported by the work of Robertson *et al* (2003) whose study of people in their sixties found that the group with the highest levels of life satisfaction and well being were those in part-time work, suggesting both that better work-life balance is important, and that a degree of control over one's life has positive benefits for the individual.

Chapter 8
Volunteers, social policy and adult learning

Peter Lavender

Summary

This chapter explores the nature of voluntary work in adult learning, taking as its starting point the first adult literacy campaign in the 1970s. Using a study of volunteers from 1989 I attempt to place the first campaign in a broader context. A number of social policy 'streams' were in evidence then, including 'active citizenship'; individual responsibility to care for others; the State's responsibility to fill the gaps left by individual, volunteer and voluntary sector support; and the idea of national community service. It is not suggested that thirty years later the position is the same. However, some parallels can be usefully made with the present Government interest in volunteering. In 2004 Gordon Brown, Chancellor of the Exchequer, set up a commission on volunteering during a speech to the NCVO, in advance of the 'year of volunteering' in 2005. Later, in a budget speech he set aside £150 million to develop a 'national strategy for volunteering', particularly among young adults (Shifrin, 2004). In addition, there has been some recognition that volunteers are also adult learners (Swinney, 2005). The learning that volunteers do is a strong and recurring theme in Veronica McGivney's work. It appeared in her work on pre-schools, in *'Fixing or Changing the Pattern'* (2001) and in much of her work on widening participation since 1988.

Looking to the past

A look back at the first adult literacy campaign in the early 1970s is a good starting point (Hamilton and Hillier, 2006). As we approach 2007 and the target of a million learners passing a national qualification in basic skills, it is worth remembering that *Skills for Life* is our second national campaign on literacy in England, not the first. There is a major difference between then and now. Thirty years ago what the journalists wrote about frequently was the involvement of volunteers as teachers (Mares, 1975; Hill, 1976). The use of teaching volunteers in educational provision for adults became widespread during the first Adult Literacy Campaign, reaching a peak of activity between 1975 and 1977. Some 31,437 volunteers were recorded as teaching in adult literacy in England and Wales in February 1979 (ALU, 1980). This excludes the 5,919 on waiting lists or carrying out other duties, or those teaching numeracy or English for Speakers of Other Languages. The same report to the Secretary of State mentions that there were 69,470 literacy students being taught, and less than 4,000 full- and part-time staff. The scale of volunteer involvement in this area was unprecedented; it seems appropriate to reflect on this at the time of writing in the Year of the Volunteer (2005).

Not only was the scale of volunteering unusual but it also raised important questions. In 1981 the National Institute of Adult Education carried out a review of existing research in adult and continuing education in relation to the voluntary sector (Withnall, Osborn and Charnley, 1981). There was 'a dearth of research in this topic area', they noted, but of particular interest to me was this suggestion for further research:

> . . . we need to know not only about the individual motivation of volunteers but also something of the ways in which the organisations in which they work harness (or fail to harness) the motives of the volunteers to their own goals'. (Withnall, Osborn and Charnley, 1981, p. 76)

The suggestion is that volunteers in adult literacy are no different to other volunteers working in the public sector, and that without knowing what motivates them it is difficult to ensure that they obtain the benefits and satisfactions they need or expect. It also raises the question of how to manage volunteers effectively and to understand the nature of their individual motivation. Later, two research studies would recognise volunteering as learning (Elsey and Gibbs, 1981; ACACE, 1983), a theme to which more than one publication (see for example Darrill *et al*, 1998; Swinney, 2005) has returned.

But at the time that volunteers were such a major force in adult education there were many social policy 'streams' which wove volunteers into the plot, each with different ideological underpinnings. For example, volunteers were seen in relation to the changing view of young people and of the Welfare State, unemployment, and national community service. The image of voluntary work shifted in 1979 from, 'a middle class voluntary, altruistic, initiative' to an 'industry felt appropriate for working class youngsters' (Allinson, 1978, p. 7). Volunteer bureaux flourished and the period between 1960 and 1979 was described as a 'volunteer boom' (Aves, 1969). Evidence of a 'dual benefit' theory (benefit to individuals and to those they help) can be seen in how projects and organisations moved from a service *by* youth to a service *for* youth, a shift which was to be repeated in the community work element of Government training schemes in the 1980s. In 1981 Youth Call attempted to return to the dual benefit notion. Youth Call suggested a national youth volunteering service, based on work that needed doing. Those involved in Youth Call had set up organisations in the 1960s such as Task Force, the Young Volunteer Force Foundation and Community Service Volunteers. It was during the 1960s that the infrastructure of volunteering was developed and national agencies like the Volunteer Centre UK and Voluntary Services Unit were created.

As 'voluntary work' became 'community service' it was sometimes seen as a mechanism for the social control of young people in the 'moral panic' which followed 'sit-ins', 'mods and rockers' and rebellion (Finn, 1987; Varlaam, 1984; Cohen, 1973). Community service in the school curriculum became significant after the school leaving age was raised to 16 (1973) when young people themselves were often seen as the problem. The 'experience curriculum' developed into 'work experience' as unemployment rose sharply in 1974. Work experience for school leavers was also regarded as a means of 'remotivating' and occupying young people, and separating them from adult status (Stronach, 1984; Watts, 1983). Vocational preparation initiatives like the Youth Opportunities Programme (1978) rose in importance at this time.

Characteristics of volunteers in literacy work

Against this background came the adult literacy campaign with its volunteer involvement, often managed by organisers who started as volunteers themselves. One link between the first and second literacy campaign is that many of the most senior practitioners in the second began as volunteers in the first[1]. The characteristics of those first campaign volunteers were distinctive. They were similar to other volunteers working in the statutory sector but dissimilar to the rest of the population. For instance, they were mainly women with an advantaged initial education, likely to be in employment or with young families, and middle class by occupation. In volunteer bureaux, on the other hand, volunteers were more likely to be younger, unemployed and male (Lavender, 1989)[2]. There was an identifiable population likely to volunteer in adult literacy and they were slightly different from the general population and from those attracted into voluntary work through volunteer bureaux. Voluntary work was also occurring for volunteers at significant moments in adulthood (Beugen, 1985); and some of these moved on to careers and training as a direct result of their voluntary work. Very few literacy volunteers said they wanted to pursue careers in teaching. There are implications here for volunteers as adult learners and for training and development practices (Swinney, 2005).

The reasons people volunteer are many and fascinating, as Titmuss outlined in his 1970 study of why people give blood (Titmuss, 1970). The issue of motivation, I believe, moves voluntary work into the moral domain. In reality, what I found in my 1989 study (Lavender, 1989) was that volunteers were rarely asked why they wanted to help. They also felt unable to mention their real reasons. What organisers wanted to hear was all about reciprocity, that volunteers were doing it for themselves. This unease about motives in general, with the organisers suspicious of altruism and the volunteers unhappy about motives of self-interest, raises questions about the notion of reciprocity. A better definition of altruism as 'concern for the weal of another person as a principle of action' would make a difference to the way organisers and volunteers view voluntary work. It is also a definition which can displace the commonly-viewed idea of altruism as noble self-sacrifice. Such an 'other-regarding' definition has a long history and was rediscovered in Abrams' 1979 study of neighbouring.

Although the prevailing explanation of motivation among volunteers appears to be based on models of social exchange or reciprocity, the norm as far as volunteers were concerned was beneficence, prompted by altruistic feelings of wanting to help others. At the base of organisers' fears of this 'norm of beneficence' must be the risk associated with unequal power relationships and the students' feelings. The same disquiet is often felt about voluntary work as 'gift-giving'. In other words, to protect the recipients' feelings may have been to deny the volunteers' feelings. Abrams' (1979) solution was to acknowledge the altruistic motive but to manage volunteers through their other 'causal' reasons (such as having spare time), but this approach was often rejected by literacy organisers because of the risk of manipulation. Far better, it might be argued, to explore the other-regarding nature of altruism openly with volunteers and organisers and then to focus on the needs and interests of volunteers themselves rather than to see them as a means to an (organisational) end. It is a short step from this suggestion to view volunteers as partners in an act of learning; they about learning to help and the students about learning to improve their literacy skills; both partners involved in a study of the nature of adult learning.

It was not to be. The dominant theme in the first literacy campaign was that volunteers added a great deal of freshness, bringing new people in to work in the literacy field. But volunteers were really a means to an end. Very little attention was paid by organisers to the management of volunteer motivation. 'We have not cared for them' said one organiser. The reason for this may be because the organisers felt that their first responsibility was to the students rather than volunteers. This split of responsibility can be seen at national level too, in the differences in tone between the way in which the Volunteer Centre UK and the Adult Literacy and Basic Skills Unit (ALBSU) spoke of support for volunteers. The former referred to responsibilities owed to volunteers, and the latter about ensuring that volunteers are *effective* (Lavender, 1989, pp. 187–195).

In the first literacy campaign organisers felt they had no choice about whether they used volunteers or not. 'It was a given,' said one (Lavender, 1989). This led to an undercurrent of suspicion by volunteers that they were being used simply as a cheap way of giving individual tuition. The managerial styles adopted by organisers tended to confirm this. Organisers' assumptions about volunteers' motivation, together with their own beliefs and experiences, sometimes as a volunteer, created a rather traditional managerial climate in literacy work. Volunteers were rarely required to contribute opinions or decision-making skills, and the evaluation process and running of the organisation was entirely in the hands of the organisers (ACACE, 1983, p. 42). Although organisers subscribed to a model of student participation in which the goal of student empowerment was a common theme, this did not often extend to their view of volunteers:

> The tragedy of all this waste is that much of the job satisfaction
> of professionals could be solved if they involved volunteers . . .
> Volunteers can reciprocally be highly supportive of paid staff,
> they provide professionals with a new kind of team experi-
> ence . . . (Bruce and Darvill, 1967, p. 295)

The role of volunteers as a form of support for literacy organisers would have repaid further research. In the first literacy campaign the training provided to volunteers could be described as a process of 'professionalisation' in which volunteers were regarded as part-time unpaid staff or as learners but never as volunteers in their own right; apprentices learning the 'tools of the trade' but not partners in an educational community. 'I found myself able to crystallise several half understood points about myself as pupil or tutor', one volunteer noted (Lavender, 1989, p. 554).

If volunteers had all been regarded as adult learners in their own right it may have helped the organisers to manage them differently. The organisers might have found it more comfortable to assist volunteers to develop themselves through voluntary work. This in turn might have enabled the volunteers to feel more individually valued by organisers; would mean that their reasons for volunteering could be discussed; and what they learned could be reviewed on a regular and mutually rewarding basis. In addition the students might genuinely feel that they were partners in co-learning. But this is speculation, and creating such an organisational climate would bring with it three challenges. First, finding the resources to allow as much time for organisers to support volunteers as they do their students. Second, addressing the shift of expectations among volunteers from 'helping' to 'being helped'. Third, recognising in policy terms that voluntary work was not a 'cheap option'. None of these issues was insurmountable but all seemed so at the time. As one text put it:

> The ABE organiser needs to develop a full personal awareness of the learning which is going on in the organisation. This is a task of personal recognition and analysis. Are people discovering major new dimensions to their lives, perhaps to coincide with changes in life circumstances? The organiser's own effort to recognise and analyse the learning activities in the organisation is likely to highlight the importance of these in contributing to the effectiveness of the organisation. (Darvill, Perkins and Unell, 1988, p. 33)

Literacy volunteers and social policy

Volunteers, it is argued, have been used in literacy work in the past as a means to an end, perhaps as unpaid staff or at the very least as trainees or apprentices, but this was not peculiar to literacy work since volunteers have also been 'used' on the macro level by social policy makers in order to support political rhetoric. In neither case have adult volunteers been intended as the main beneficiaries.

Social policy is often implemented in a pragmatic fashion as opportunity arises and can seem to be the result of jumbled processes and undirected strategies that do not connect with each other. This may be because we are searching for one service policy instead of recognising a number of social policy 'streams'. Direct government support for literacy work, with 'targeted' funding, brought adult education provision into the sphere of social policy in its own right, first in 1975 and again from 2000 during the second campaign (DfES, 2001). Volunteers, however, are reflected in a different set of social policy 'streams' which can be traced back to Beveridge (1948). Such 'streams' include voluntary work in relation to the changing view of young people and of the Welfare State, unemployment, national community service, and 'active citizenship'.

The shift from 'voluntary work' to 'community service' which took place in the volunteer 'boom years' of 1960–1979 was mentioned earlier, but this was also accompanied by discontent with the costs and results of the Welfare State. Here the 'disabling' effect of the increasing number of professionals within it led to a search for a more pluralist solution during the 1970s. The 'failure of egalitarianism', together with trade union difficulties, the oil crisis, rising inflation and unemployment paved the way for sharp economies in the public sector. This led to a re-examination of the role of volunteers both at voluntary organisation and government level. During this period the first adult literacy campaign was launched (February, 1975), managed by the Adult Literacy Resource Agency (ALRA). Local education authorities (LEAs) set up structures based on voluntary sector models, with large numbers of volunteer 'tutors'. This was at a time when in most other statutory and voluntary services the relationships between volunteers and paid staff were being reviewed against a background of economic difficulty and social change. The work of the Orme Committee on exactly this subject was swept away by the 1979 Conservative election. The Thatcher government developed a 'small government' approach to the provision of public services, extended the public sector economies with enthusiasm and welcomed welfare pluralism as central to their social policy; eventually crucial in relation to policies towards mass unemployment.

The Director of the Young Volunteer Force Foundation was one of the few people on the management committee of ALRA with experience of running a national campaign; this had involved recruiting 10,000 young volunteers in less than five years. The British Association of Settlements and Cambridge House were the other two voluntary organisation representatives, each with a similarly strong and apparently unquestioned investment in the use of volunteers. Between June 1975 and June 1976 over 60,000 students and 40,000 adult literacy volunteers came forward, inspired by a series of BBC programmes.

The use of volunteers was relatively novel to local education authorities in 1974 (Hill, 1976). Although the decision to use volunteers appeared to be 'accidental', five distinct pressures resulted in their use becoming standard practice in all but one LEA. First, the haste with which the Campaign was launched. The £1 million government grant for 1974–75 and 1975–76 was announced in July 1974, leaving the national unit responsible for disbursing the money already four months into the first financial year. Pressure from the BBC Project between November 1973 and September 1975, when the referral service was established and the first programmes started, had built up enormous expectations and momentum. There was little time to recruit paid staff or question the use of volunteers. Second, most of the expertise lay in the voluntary sector. Because LEAs were led to believe that individual tuition was a necessary condition, they could see no way of delivering such a service without volunteers. Third, LEAs had just been reorganised and public sector expenditure cuts were biting hard. Few LEAs could have afforded to pay the costs of so many new, paid staff. Fourth, the BBC Project had a major influence on LEAs since it was some time before the Resource Agency was operating and there was little authoritative national advice except from BBC briefings and newsletters. The BBC Project strongly favoured volunteers, often making no distinction between paid and voluntary tutors (BBC, 1974; Hargreaves, 1977). Finally, there was an assumption in the media that most of the teaching would be done by the volunteers, often working one-to-one at home.

Provision for adult literacy work developed into adult basic education (ABE) provision, reflecting the broader interest in numeracy, English for speakers of other languages, provision for adults with disabilities, and so forth. This can be seen in the report of the Advisory Council for Adult and Continuing Education (ACACE, 1979). The significance of the volunteers, heralded a few years earlier, was played down at this time. The 'professionalisation' of the workforce was thought to be impeded by the emphasis on volunteers. Then, as now, there were shortages of professional staff, battles on the ratio between paid and volunteer tutors, an unwillingness to invest in adult education infrastructure, and the Government's 'small government' approach (Wilenski, 1986). In addition, policy makers frequently blurred any distinction between 'voluntary organisations' and statutory organisations using 'volunteers'; both were often regarded as 'voluntary'.

One example of such blurring can be seen in the confidential report from the Central Policy Review Staff which was strongly supported by the Number 10 Policy Unit (Rose, 1983). It recommended to the Cabinet in 1981 more community service for adults in return for benefits plus expenses, a compulsory youth training year for all unemployed school leavers, reduced training wages, lower wages for young employees, and entry to the job market raised to the age of 17. All these measures were eventually implemented under the Conservative Government. After riots in the summer of 1981, one particular £8 million government scheme, the Voluntary Projects Programme (VPP), was announced by the Prime Minister. The scheme was intended to reduce the potentially damaging energies of unemployed young people and to give them worthwhile voluntary work in return for benefits plus expenses. It took more than a year for the Manpower Services Commission (MSC) to find a way of fitting such a programme into their training objectives. This they did by changing the emphasis from benefit to the community to benefit to oneself, and later introduced an element of training and work preparation. The 'volunteers' were the participants.

Voluntary work in return for benefits

The VPP is significant in this story for three reasons. First, it paved the way for schemes of training and work for unemployed adults in return for benefits plus expenses or a low allowance, as developed later in Employment Training and the Youth Training Scheme (1988). This has evolved into the mandatory studying of basic skills as part of the Job Centre Plus arrangements (Joyce *et al*, 2005). In the past, schemes for adults and young people had tended to be about work experience and had offered a training allowance well above benefits level. The VPP was an example of the move to occupy 'idle hands' usefully. Although implementation involved training and skills acquisition another outcome intended was the experiment of giving work to unemployed people in exchange for benefits and basic skills training. Second, VPP linked for the first time basic skills, unemployment and volunteering. This link was to be used later in the Job Training Scheme and Employment Training, and more recently in efforts to reduce the number of adults on incapacity benefit. In 1981 the MSC encouraged education providers, mostly LEAs, to sponsor VPP schemes. This in turn changed the traditional definition of 'volunteer' as someone working for others without financial reward, to someone working to improve their own skills and solely for their own benefit – a shift from volunteer to trainee, in fact. Adult literacy or ABE remained one of the VPP's main elements in all MSC literature. The third reason for the VPP's importance is that it was an example of social policy ostensibly created for one purpose when others were clearly intended. For example, the announcement by the Prime Minister about VPP was assumed to be in response to the riots but in fact the Cabinet had already heard that voluntary work was,

> . . . a more justifiable – and much more cost-effective – measure than support for some of the lame duck industries which consume energy and materials . . . (CPRS Report, quoted in Rose, 1983, p. 6)

The genesis of VPP lay in the Cabinet discussions around the Central Policy Review Staff (CPRS) paper of February 1981 (Rose, 1983) or even in the comments of Home Office ministers, James Prior and Lord Gowrie, in July 1980. In June 1981, 'enabling' regulations, allowing volunteers to claim unemployment benefits while undertaking voluntary work, were pushed through at the Department of Health and Social Security by Patrick Jenkin.

Further policy intent towards volunteers can be seen in elements of the Cabinet's views in the Employment White Paper at the time (HMSO, 1981) on 'A New Training Initiative'. Thwarted by the MSC and their need for consensus among trade unions, employers and voluntary organisations, the CPRS recommendations emerged next in the 'Benefit Plus' proposals in March 1982. Again, the MSC amended the proposals to include, for instance, higher allowances than 'benefit plus' and the Community Programme was launched in October 1982. The Cabinet's desire to offer 'benefits only' to adults in order for them to do voluntary work had been intended in February 1981, announced in July and implemented, at least in part, through the VPP in August 1982. It was to be seven years before the Government could fully implement the policy intentions first identified in 1981. Parallel to the Government's 'benefit plus' direction, and possibly a strong influence on it, was the pressure at the time for national community service.

National community service

Since 1981 the national community service debate firmly linked voluntary work to unemployment and young people. The argument was that community service, equated with 'volunteering' as we have seen above, would have seven benefits. These were: reduced alienation; the learning of new skills; a mixing together of young people; improved level of social and welfare services; removal of young people from the labour market; a break between school and higher education; and more socially-aware citizens. The various schemes for national voluntary service were linked by some of the same public figures. The arguments put forward as to why such a scheme was necessary usually revolved around there being 'a crisis of care', work that needed to be done in the public sector which could not be afforded otherwise, or the need to harness the enthusiasm of altruistic young people. Rarely mentioned were the darker sides: high unemployment or the control of youth behaviours. Separate schemes were proposed by Youth Call, the Social Democratic Party, Conservative backbenchers, the Tawney Society, the Association of Directors of Social Services, the directors of Community Service Volunteers and of the Women's Royal Voluntary Service, and Prince Charles.

Arguments against national community service have focused on philosophy, job substitution, finance/allowances, and choice. Neuman (1985) suggested that a national scheme of volunteering would have to be run by the Training Agency whose objectives were not service to the Welfare State, but training; a fact which so changed the VPP. In addition, voluntary organisations might become more centrally controlled (Simmonds, 1988), the placement might undermine paid jobs in the public sector, the State might be able to avoid some responsibility for services, and the concept may lead to unemployed people having to work for their benefits. In the United States, Senator Nunn introduced a Bill in 1988 which allowed young people doing voluntary work to 'earn' the equivalent of university fees. Some writers like Slipman (1986) and Walker (1989) urged that rewards for volunteers doing community service, such as certification and accreditation, were more acceptable to them than altruistic feeling (Murphy, 1985; Wolmar, 1984). In 1987 Prince Charles joined the debate, to be followed by Youth Call's (1981) proposals that national community service should be voluntary, certificated and encourage 'active citizenship' (Commission on Youth, 1981). The fear was that simplistic solutions such as compulsory service for those unemployed and unskilled could damage the positive nature of voluntary involvement.

It at first seemed unlikely that community service would be suggested as part of the Government's 'active citizenship' strategy since Section 4 of the 1988 Social Security Act effectively removed sixteen- and seventeen-year-olds from the labour market. Those not attending the Youth Training Scheme were no longer offered benefits. The Department of Employment seemed unlikely to want to move back to community service schemes from training for skills and the Government appeared unlikely to implement a scheme which could be politically unpopular, when the social policy goals of reducing young people's wages and 'benefits plus' training had been implemented by other means. Nevertheless, the national community service debate had an important place in the late 1980s. It seemed to achieve strong support from the public and the Conservative and centre parties, and it supported the Conservative Government's view that voluntary work should be an alternative to unemployment. What made the concept even more powerful from 1988 onwards was the swift way the lobbyists changed the national community service argument into one which accommodated the Conservative notion of 'active citizenship'.

Active citizenship

In September 1988 the Government's Party Conference was dominated by the concept of 'active citizenship'. This coincided with the introduction of the final element of the CPRS recommendations: a national youth training scheme for 16–18 year olds with a low training allowance, no benefits for those refusing a place, a 'benefits plus' national adult training programme with a low (£10 per week) allowance on top of benefits (first seen in VPP) and a voluntary work option for those leaving such schemes. 'Active citizenship' exemplified all the elements underpinning the implementation of Government social policy at the time: market mechanisms, competition favouring the voluntary and private sectors, individualism and individual choice, minimum state provision of welfare services, and individuals, families, businesses and 'active citizens' taking the lead to 'look after their own'.

There are several social policy streams which affect or relate to volunteering but 'active citizenship' appears to be the first explicit central government policy towards volunteering itself. Home Secretary Douglas Hurd's belief at the time was that 'neighbourliness' would be the 'political test' of the 1990s (Perera, 1988). He suggested that voluntary work was an obligation of increasing affluence and brought a return to 'Victorian values' and a means of promoting social cohesion. If 'active citizenship' was the 'lynchpin of Thatcher's Britain' (*The Guardian*, 1988) its significance extends beyond one social policy stream. The roots of 'active citizenship' as a concept lie in the Conservative Party's 'traditional beliefs' in service and order, but its use by Government ministers at this time seems to have four purposes. First, it was an attempt to 'capture the moral high ground' of politics. 'Active citizens' are moral citizens and their work is underpinned by what another

Home Office minister described as 'the moral imperative' (Patten, 1988). Baker (1988) and others argued that the Conservative Party was the party which protected absolute moral values such as honesty and care for others. Second, Government rhetoric since 1979 had favoured moral individual and family responsibility, business in the community and less State involvement in welfare provision. The aim appeared to be to underpin social policy with a moral rationale. 'Active citizenship', the argument goes, justified a reduction of State welfare provision on moral grounds, enabling government policy to be based on moral views rather than political dogma, and helped to 'roll back the frontiers of the State' by keeping State provision to a minimum. Third, governments between 1979 and 1989 had a coherent ideology based on market principles, which they applied to the Welfare State. It was argued that individualism and individual choice was important in this and that wealth enabled citizens to enjoy 'new-found freedom' through giving to charity and doing voluntary work. Finally, 'active citizenship' usually presaged an attack on supposed Labour paternalism, the 'statism' of the past, spectres of bureaucracy and insensitivity, the so-called 'nanny state' and those who recommended increased State provision of services.

Some of these four purposes of 'active citizenship' involve assumptions based on very little apparent evidence: that increased wealth means increased voluntary work, that voluntary workers and voluntary organisations are more effective than professional workers, and that market forces lead to a better and more just society. Other challenges begin with definitions of citizenship. The Government at the time attempted to overturn traditional definitions of citizenship based on rights. This 'market citizenship' omits the essential element of the citizen's rights – unrelated to wealth, class or family background. Meanings change, as in the word 'altruism', but 'active citizenship' could not alter the traditional meaning of citizenship as a 'citizenship of rights' unless there was widespread acceptance of the new definition, and there was not.

Conclusion

Against this background, adult literacy volunteers can be seen as 'active citizens' in the Government's definition of the time. They tended to be more comfortably off, middle class and educated to a higher level than most of the population. Similar kinds of people volunteered for adult literacy, later ABE, as for most other volunteer activities in statutory services and their characteristics have remained unchanged since the Aves Report (1969).

Although there has been a massive increase in students learning adult literacy and other basic skills since 1979, there has been a steady decrease in the number of volunteers required, presumably because of the 'professional-isation' of the service offered. They now number about 10,000. Against the background of the citizenship debate it is possible to see how literacy work, firmly in the social policy arena, was as much affected by Government support as any other part of the statutory sector which used volunteers to achieve its objectives.

The concept of 'citizenship' has altered over time and through changing governments and policies. However, many of the concepts from earlier years remain – the idea that altruism has to include self sacrifice and is to be frowned on, the notion that 'personalisation' is unique to the current government, that volunteers are a major force for improving the services offered to individuals and communities, and that young people volunteering should be encouraged. New concepts of citizenship are required as govern-ments change. It was the Commission on Citizenship as far back as 1989 which recommended that 'citizenship' should be taught in every secondary school and all pupils should complete a nationally recognised community service course which would carry status and a record of achievement. Recently, the Green Paper on Youth, *Youth Matters* (HMSO, 2005) following the Russell Commission's recommendations, proposed providing reward points for volunteering and encouragement for thousands more young people to volunteer. Russell noted that it was not credit young people wanted but real personal enrichment:

> The strong message I got from young people we spoke to is that they saw voluntary work as something that they wanted to do because of its benefits. (Russell, 2006)

The echo from debates in the 1980s is still sharp but what seems like a cyclical return to issues of volunteering, young people and citizenship is arresting. In the case of adult literacy, though, the moment has probably passed when a renewed interest in large-scale volunteering might return. For those organisers and education providers who might consider, perhaps as a kind of apprenticeship, introducing volunteers to work in adult literacy, numeracy or language work, there are some messages. First, the need for a recognition that a very particular group of people volunteer in statutory organisations; and that this group can be widened but it ought to be valued too. Second, that their motivation for joining in is likely to be from a norm of beneficence and that the incidence of volunteering may not reflect the level of need in an area. It is also important to establish how such motivation is to be managed. Third, promoting the concept of volunteering and citizenship, active or otherwise, does not alter the fact that successful involvement of volunteers depends not on their individual wealth or Government exhortation, but on the motivations of individuals and on how much support they receive in their volunteering. Finally, a Government's wish to promote volunteering (or 'active citizenship') may not be to increase voluntary activity but to justify social policy and claim a 'moral high ground'. There are several commentators who acknowledge the links between social policy in the 1980s and today. Johnson and Steinberg (2005) observe that in many ways 'Blairism' is Thatcher's legacy.

The cycle has not quite come full circle but it is looking that way. We now have mandatory basic skills training for those receiving benefits. Gordon Brown is urging the expansion of military cadet forces, 'especially in state schools' (Luckhurst, 2006), and the use of voluntary work to create more active citizens:

> . . . in fact when a recent Mori poll showed that 59 per cent of 15 to 24 year olds want to know more about how to get involved in their communities... I believe we have a goodwill mountain just waiting to be tapped. The advantages for young people are clear – to develop their personal skills, discover new communities, become more active citizens. The benefits to our country are clear too: to expand volunteering, to create a culture of service and to support worthwhile community activity. And as in America there could be help with basic living expenses and help for university, college or business start ups to follow. Service can make us a stronger, more caring, more resilient society. (Brown, 2004)

We are receiving similar messages to those noted during the 'active citizenship' era. A national strategy for volunteering, focused on young people, may (just as before) spill over into other age groups and purposes. Meanwhile, £150 million is a clear indicator of its importance. It remains to be seen whether the new national volunteer strategy is regarded as a learning experience for those involved. There is no mention, as yet.

References

Abrams, P. (1979) *Altruism and Reciprocity: Altruism as Reciprocity*, Working Paper ii, Durham: University of Durham, Rowntree Research Group

ACACE (1979) *A Strategy for the Basic Education of Adults*, Leicester: ACACE

ACACE (1983) *Volunteers in Adult Education*, Advisory, Leicester: ACACE

Allinson, C. (1978) *Young Volunteers?* A Community Projects Foundation Community Work and Youth Work Paper, London: Community Projects Foundation

ALU (1980) *Adult Literacy: 1978/79*. Report to the Secretary of State for Education and Science and the Secretary of State for Wales by the Adult Literacy Unit's Management Committee on the First Year of Operation, London: HMSO

Aves (1969) *The Voluntary Worker in the Social Services*, Originally published as NISWT series No. 16 and NCSS Publication 787. Berkhamsted: The Volunteer Centre.

Baker, K. (1988) Speech of 8th November, reported in *New Statesman and Society*, 16th December 1988, p. 28, repeated in a speech to the Synod, January 1989

BBC (1974) *Adult Literacy Project*, letter to local education authorities, November 1974. London: BBC

Beugen, P. J. (1985) 'Supporting the Volunteer Life-Cycle', *Voluntary Action Leadership*, Fall: 17–19

Beveridge, W. (1942) *Social Insurance and Allied Services*, Cmnd 6404. London: His Majesty's Stationery Office

Brown, G. (2004) Gordon Brown's speech to NCVO Annual Conference. Available at http://www.ncvo-vol.org.uk/events/speeches/?id=1266. Last accessed 17 March 2006

Bruce, I. and Darvill, G. (1967) 'Over the defences: the volunteer in the area team' in *Social Work Today*, 7(9): 294–296

Cohen, S. (1973) *Folk Devils and Moral Panics*, London: Paladin

Commision on Youth (1981) *Commision on Youth and the Needs of the Nation*, unpublished document, London: Commission on Youth.

Darvill, G., Perkins, E. and Unell, J. (1988) *Learning from Volunteering: An Exploratory Study*. Leicester: Unit for the Development of Adult Continuing Education/ National Institute for Adult Continuing Education

DfES (2001) *Skills for Life: The National Strategy for Improving Literacy and Numeracy Skills*, London: DfES

Elsey, B. and Gibbs, M. (1981) *Voluntary Tutors in Adult Literacy: A Survey of Adult Literacy Volunteers in the Nottingham Area* Nottingham Working Papers in the Education of Adults No. 3, Nottingham: Department of Adult Education, University of Nottingham

Finn, D. (1987) *Training Without Jobs*, Basingstoke: Macmillan Education

The Guardian (1988) 'Political Totem or Society's Cement – the Active Citizen is the Lynchpin of Thatcher's Britain. What kind of Person Fits the Label?' *The Guardian*, Wednesday 9th November 1988, page 21

Hamilton, M. and Hillier, Y. (2006) *Changing Faces of Adult Literacy, Language and Numeracy: A Critical History*, Stoke-on-Trent: Trenham Books. Also available at http://www.lancs.ac.uk/fss/projects/edres/changingfaces. Last accessed 17 March 2006

Hargreaves, D. (1977) *On the Move: The BBC's Contribution to the Adult Literacy Campaign in the United Kingdom Between 1972 and 1976*. London: BBC Education.

Hill, F. (1976) 'Keen, But Can They Teach . . . ?' *The Times Educational Supplement*, Friday 4th June 1976, p. 8.

HMSO (1981) *A New Training Initiative: A Programme for Action*. Cmnd 8455. London: HMSO

HMSO (2005) *Youth Matters* Cmnd 6629 July 2005. Norwich: HMSO

Russell, I. (2006) Quoted in *Young People Now*. Available at http://www.ypnmagazine.com/news/index.cfm?fuseaction=full_news&ID=9097. Last accessed 4 January 2006

Joyce, L., Durham, J., Williams, M. and White, C. (2005) *Evaluation of*

Basic Skills Mandatory Training Pilots and National Enhancements Interim Report Research Report No. 307, BMRB for Department of Work and Pensions, London: HMSO

Lavender, P. R. S. (1989) *Volunteers in Adult Basic Education*, unpublished PhD thesis, Centre for Applied Research in Education, University of East Anglia.

Luckhurst, T. (2006) Education section of *The Independent*, Thursday 16 March 2006

Mares, C. (1975) 'Steps to saintliness', *Times Educational Supplement*, 12 December 1975, p. 55

McGivney, V. (2001) *Fixing or Changing the Pattern?* Leicester: NIACE

Murphy, F. (1985) Speech to 'Count Us In' conference held at London School of Economics, Saturday 16th March 1985 and reported in *Involve*, No. 43, May 1985, pp. 1–2

Neuman, H. (1985) 'Beyond community service, the spectre of enslavement', *Involve* No. 43, May 1985, pp. 2–3

Patten, J. (1988) 'Launching the active citizen', *The Guardian*, Wednesday 28th September 1988

Patten, J. (1988) 'The active citizen viewed from left to right' in *Involve*, 60(Autumn): 6–7

Perera, S. (1988) 'Hurd hints at paid time off for voluntary workers', *The Guardian*, Monday 19 September, p. 3

Rose, D. (1983) 'Thatcher's secret unemployment plans', *Time Out*, 20–26 May, pp. 5–7

Shifrin, T. (2004) 'Brown outlines national volunteer strategy', *The Guardian*, Wednesday 17 March

Simmonds, D. (1988) 'Editorial: Employment training – the challenge to research', *ARVAC Bulletin* No. 34, Autumn 1988

Slipman, S. (1986) 'The case for a national volunteer scheme', *Youth in Society*, 118 (September): 9

Steinberg, D. and Johnson, R. (2005) *Blairism and the War of Persuasion: Labour's Passive Revolution*, London: Lawrence and Wishart

Stronach, I. (1984) 'Work experience: the sacred anvil' in Varlaam, C. (ed.) *Rethinking Transition: Educational Innovation and the Transition to Adult Life*. Lewes: The Falmer Press

Swinney, J. (2005) *Volunteers and Volunteering, Lifelines in Adult Learning 14*, Leicester: NIACE

Titmuss, R.M. (1970) *The Gift Relationship – From Human Blood to Social Policy*, London: George Allen and Unwin

Varlaam, C. (ed.) (1984) *Rethinking Transition: Educational Innovation and the Transition to Adult Life*, Lewes: The Falmer Press

Walker, M. (1989) 'Volunteers for the young idea in America', *The Guardian*, Wednesday 8 February, p. 23

Watts, A.G. (1983) *Work Experience and Schools*, London: Heinemann

Wilenski, P. (1986) *Public Power and Public Administration*, Sydney: Hale and Iremonger/Royal Australian Institute of Public Administration

Withnall, A., Osborn, M. and Charnley, A.H. (1981) *Review of Existing Research in Adult and Continuing Education. Volume V: The Voluntary Field*, Leicester: NIACE

Wolmar, C. (1984) 'Youth Call: round two', *Voluntary Action*, November: p. 7

Notes

[1] For an excellent historical account see Hamilton and Hillier, 2006.
[2] The study was based on surveys of volunteers in adult basic education and in a volunteer bureau, interviews with organisers in four contexts and in six other statutory services.

Chapter 9

Kennedy revisited: we know how to widen participation – now we need to make it happen

Judith Summers

People in non-participant categories have a widespread tendency to equate all forms of learning with formal school education . . . The surveys conducted during the project revealed considerable anger and hostility towards a system which was widely seen as trying to impose and uphold the values of a particular social class and culture. Thus, the major barriers to participation are attitudes, perceptions and expectations . . . For their part, people working in education tend to regard non-participants as the 'problem', rather than exploring how the system itself has failed to be relevant and attractive to a large proportion of the adult population . . . The argument for widening access should not be polarised into either traditional adult provision or work with new groups, but should make the case for a more flexible, multi-targeted service, operating from the recognition that the community is composed of different groups with equally valid learning interests and requirements. (McGivney, 1990)

Over the past fifteen years or so, NIACE's work has been underpinned by a simple belief: that not only more, but different, adults should be able to participate in learning. Two research strands have been essential to making the case: the quantitative work of its authoritative participation surveys, and the series of studies which Veronica McGivney has carried out, alongside the work of the Replan and UDACE units. The quotation above is from *Education's for Other People*, the title of her ESRC-funded research which has taken on a life of its own, and it encapsulates what is important about the work. Tackling attitudinal barriers to participation was then politically fraught for many, because it could seem to come close to the 'on your bike' outlook, the preference in government circles for blaming the victims of unemployment and exclusion. The trenchancy with which McGivney defined the problem was liberating and, I believe, influential. This essay follows the theme in the work of the Kennedy Committee, which reported in 1997 on widening participation in further education, and looks at a particular proposal for a 'more flexible, multi-targeted service'. It suggests that the recognition 'that the community is composed of different groups with equally valid learning interests' has yet to be fully accepted in public policy.

The Committee's report, *Learning Works* (Kennedy, 1997) had an interesting gestation. The Committee was set up in late 1994 to advise the Further Education Funding Council on how it could promote access, and took some time to get its bearings and to be satisfied with its evidence base. As work progressed, it became apparent that to publish before the next general election, which it was assumed Labour would win, would ensure that the conclusions lacked impact. However, there was widespread interest from the field, where practitioners were waiting for recognition and support for their work – not least because of the profile which the access movement had given to the challenge of participation, and the networks which committee members used to feed in experience and live issues. Expectations were if anything increased by the publication of the visionary Tomlinson report on inclusive learning late in 1996 (FEFC, 1996). The Committee needed to demonstrate that it had something to offer and to position itself.

It therefore published its 'emerging conclusions' in early 1997, with two immediate recommendations. Strategic partnerships should be funded to develop joint working to widen participation locally, and a 'new learning pathway' should be introduced to provide a route through the wide range of opportunities in further education for adults (FEFC, 1997a). One commentator has suggested that there was something 'wild and improvised' in the orchestration of the Committee's work (Parry, 2001). It is certainly true that there was no reason why these rather than other recommendations should be published at this point – other than the importance of demonstrating that the Committee could and would make concrete and persuasive proposals, rooted in experience, and that it would be possible to start work on them regardless of the election.

Both proposals responded to specific problems articulated by practitioners and to understandings which the committee had forged. Participation in the further education sector (as funded by the FEFC) could not be understood without reference to other providers such as LEA adult education services or to opportunities for informal learning in communities or through other services. Learners' needs could not be served without recognising the crucial importance of informal learning or understanding the complex journeys which could be made (both key themes in McGivney's work). The proposals attempted to tackle the corresponding barriers.

The 'strategic partnerships' were about the organisational challenge to widening participation which was presented by intense competition between institutions and by a multiplicity of sources of funding for development such as the Single Regeneration Budget, so that opportunities for re-entry to learning were chancy and often short-lived. In effect the partnerships were to replicate the work of the Committee locally in analysing local data, so as to produce a 'participation plan' which would involve all relevant partners collaborating to improve 'access, success and progress'. This proposal was carried out, with some modifications. It felt right, one might say, and in tune with the 'third way' much touted at the start of the New Labour administration.

The 'new learning pathway', arguably amongst the most radical of the Committee's recommendations, fell through, although the proposal was rooted in real experience and welcomed enthusiastically by many practitioners. The Committee's remit was to recommend how the FEFC's strategies, including the funding methodology, should be developed 'both to increase, and to improve the quality of participation'. The pathway proposal was essentially about the quality – from the learner's point of view.

A characteristic experience of many adult learners, unlike the 16–19 age group, is to start with one course, add others at the same time or later, and gradually build up (all being well) a portfolio of qualifications which would help them move on to further learning or to a job. Along the way there may be false starts and interruptions, in which attitudinal barriers as McGivney described them will be significant. For the 16–19 age group a college would expect to have a tutorial system and this was reflected in the level of funding for full-time courses. But if an adult enrols on an IT course, an evening GCSE course and an adult education course, apparently for leisure interests, the system might not even recognise that it was the same person. No one might know what her intentions might be, or that she might well need support or advice about how to complete her personal learning package. Equally, much of the 'learning gain' in this sort of journey is not formally recognised in the way that it would be on say an access to higher education course. Nor did the then funding methodology recognise the costs of meeting such needs. It was a testament to the vision and commitment of some institutions that they created and funded support systems from pre-entry to moving on to see learners through such circumstances.

The new learning pathway drew on the experience of access courses, but its aim was to improve access to existing courses and to the mainstream of further education, rather than creating an alternative curriculum. It proposed a means of tackling the barriers of 'attitudes, perceptions and expectations'. The challenge was precisely as McGivney described it: to avoid polarising provision and to make the system work better in the interests of different learners. As *Learning Works* noted:

> The 'Pathways for Learning'. . . are not yet more qualifications to be showered upon a system already overburdened with them in all shapes and sizes. The 'Pathways' represent a commitment and a quality promise to any learner that a suitable, supported route back into learning will be available. (Kennedy, 1997, p. 8)

The heart of the proposal was to accredit guidance, tutorial and learning support, so that it could be made properly and coherently available as the 'glue' which bound learning together, and be recognised by the then funding methodology. This would reward the institutions already working in this way, and be an incentive for others to change. It seemed an elegant solution.

The pathway might better be described as a framework, to be constructed according to local needs by each institution. Pathway providers would be required to be recognised as such by the FEFC – that is, it would not be an easy road to be taken opportunistically by colleges.

- It would be designed locally to reach groups that were under-represented locally.
- It would be learner-centred and based on informed choice, with learners constructing their own programme.
- It would be multi-level: learners could choose from a portfolio of courses (in principle, everything an institution offered could be drawn on to create a coherent set of choices) and would not be confined to one level at a time.
- It would be multi-exit with a set of progression options.
- All the components would be of high quality, with attention to

appropriate teaching and assessment methods, building learners' confidence and personal skills.

- There would be a planned programme of learning support in which participants' learning gains (including personal and study skills) would be accredited.
- Institutions' learner support funds would be used to help with other costs.

Although the relationship of this to the proposed strategic partnerships is only briefly touched on in the consultation document, the link is clear enough. The case for providers working together on the pathway follows from the importance of informal learning as a starting point, and establishing the pathway would be an important element of a partnership's participation plan. Unfortunately for the pathway, the two proposals were never fully coupled together, so that the strategic partnerships lacked a commitment to it and many concentrated on the front end of access, rather than the life-cycle of learning as had been hoped.

The reaction to the proposal was interesting. Many practitioners, particularly those used to Open College Network (OCN) accreditation procedures, did not find it at all hard to understand, and some reported work which was in the spirit of the pathway. For example:

> Norwich City College of Further and Higher Education's Connections Programme provides an accessible and flexible modular curriculum both in college and in community venues. The programme has a range of personal development modules and vocational 'taster' modules. It is timetabled to fit in with school hours and learners can study full time or part time. Continual assessment procedures replace traditional tests and examinations. There are two levels to the programme and two points of entry. (FEFC, 1997c, p.25)

However, it is no secret that decision-makers found it much harder. Partly, this involved resistance to meddling with the funding methodology. The Committee was already pressing the case for a 'post code' premium for learners from disadvantaged areas, as was already happening in Wales. This was won, not without difficulty. The learning pathway proposal would require favourable recognition in the 'tariff' for funding courses. The FEFC was also asked to consider making the pathway a priority for consideration when the funding system was next reviewed. One reaction was that as some providers were obviously coping there was no need to pay them for what they were already doing, even if this was unfunded, and no financial incentive required for others to do likewise. This ignored the current drive in the system to achieve institutional funding agreements and expand further, without reference to social purpose. In the event, the pathway was 'overtaken' by the post code premium, as a senior FEFC manager put it.[1]

But opposition to funding changes was not all. With some delay, work was commissioned from NIACE and the National Open College Network on how guidance, tutorial and learning support could be accredited for the pathway. Although this report was completed by summer 1997, only an exceptional level of support from the FEFC could have enabled implementation at the start of the 1997/8 academic year, as had been intended. It is probably accurate to say that decision-makers found the report dense, highly technical and hard to get hold of (although it is hard to see how generalities would have been helpful). The specification did not seem to capture the principle of providing a means of supporting access to existing qualifications[2] and it is possible too that the apparent reliance on OCN accreditation disturbed those who thought other accreditation bodies should have the option of being involved. And in *Learning Works* itself, published in July 1997, the new learning pathway proposal was accompanied by a recommendation for a national credit framework for further education and was in a way undercut by it – perhaps evidence that the early publication was not helpful. At the first anniversary meeting of the committee, it was suggested that the idea of the learning pathway lived on as part of the work on credit accumulation.

A yet more fundamental barrier to adopting the pathway was that it required the FEFC to accept the principle that it should endorse or promote a particular proposal for curriculum change (the recommendation was explicitly to the FEFC). By contrast the credit framework proposal was a recommendation to government on which the Qualifications and Curriculum Authority would lead. The divergence between the expectations of the field and the response of decision-makers was captured in the results of the formal consultation on the Kennedy Report recommendations reported in 1998: 89 per cent (277 responses) supported the development of the new learning pathway.[3] It is interesting that the change of government did not alter the FEFC mindset.

A year later, *The Learning Age* had been published, together with a DfEE response to the Kennedy Report (DfEE, 1998) which did not mention the new learning pathway but responded positively to the credit framework proposal. The new learning pathway had, for various reasons, missed its moment. There was clearly little sense of ownership of the idea in the policy community, and it was perhaps less exciting than big ideas such as the credit framework or the University for Industry. To be sure, nothing prevented an individual institution, or a strategic partnership for that matter, from designing its own version. But the FEFC had lost this opportunity to respond to Kennedy's energising of the sector with *Learning Works*' conviction that 'we know how to widen participation – now we need to make it happen'.

Eight years on (at the time of writing) it is still the case that curriculum development for widening participation flourishes, but it depends on local commitment rather than the national impetus which the Kennedy Committee sought. There is an obvious comparison to be made with literacy and numeracy provision. Here, national policy commitment to change following the Moser Report has transformed the curriculum, increased participation, and prioritised funding – even if there are reservations about how benign aspects of the changes have been.

The Learning and Skills Council produced its own widening participation strategy in 2003 (LSC, 2003). One 'cross-cutting theme' was 'creating a learning environment for adults' and its curriculum actions were:

- Supporting work to develop an appropriate range of learning opportunities for adults, including non-accredited learning.
- Implementing the relevant proposals arising from the 21st Century Skills Strategy [that is, the 2003 White Paper].
- Working to introduce a national credit framework to provide opportunities for flexible opportunities throughout life. (LSC, 2003, p. 22. Author's comments in square brackets.)

So far, the national credit framework, now the 'Framework for Achievement', remains a policy commitment (DfES, 2005), but with agonisingly slow progress. This apart, the LSC strategy is clear that innovation is a local matter:

> Many providers are capable of achieving a greater degree of contact with target groups provided that they have the confidence they will receive appropriate support from the LSC . . . We will encourage existing providers to develop innovatory provision. We will also develop capacity in new providers where there are gaps in provision, and where there is evidence that a

> new approach is required . . . Some solutions to gaps in
> provision may lie in joint provision between providers – the
> StAR (Strategic Area Review) process provides an opportunity
> for local LSCs to engage providers in discussions about shared
> activities. (LSC, 2003, p. 18)

It is not yet possible to evaluate whether the StAR process has in fact led to
significant attention to reconfiguring what is offered in the interests of
widening participation. It seems likely that this has largely been overtaken by
the overriding priority given by government to the 14–19 age group, and its
political and funding priorities for adults of *Skills for Life* and full Level 2
qualifications, which are now the focus for 'widening participation'. Local
innovation is now constrained not so much by institutions taking the easiest
route to increase numbers, but by the effective rationing in the system which
these priorities entail.[4]

Meanwhile, programmes for widening participation which embody the new
learning pathway principles have continued to develop. This is not to say that
they are explicitly based on the proposal itself, but rather that the pathway
itself came out of principles of good practice which continue to be
applicable. Indeed, later programmes have incorporated the idea of the credit
framework. A recent study of successful work to widen participation,
intended to support the LSC's strategy, includes case studies of the curriculum at two colleges, Leicester and Newham (Champney, Davey and
Lawrence, 2005).

Leicester College described a large community-based programme with
around 1700 learners a year, 80 per cent being of Asian heritage and 80 per
cent women. The starting point is interest-based modules which develop
personal and study skills 'by stealth' and are not necessarily accredited.
These can lead into a programme combining study skills units which are
OCN accredited at levels one and two, basic skills units, and vocational
content from a mainstream curriculum area. Each participant has an
individual learning plan which selects the units relevant to her and allows
lateral as well as vertical progression.

The Newham College Access Diploma Programme (NewCAD) operates
across the college's curriculum, in an area where 70 per cent of the college's
learners attract a widening participation weighting because of levels of
poverty and unemployment. In effect the college unitised its curriculum to
provide its own credit framework (again, OCN accredited) which can be

matched to qualifications in the National Framework. At both Leicester and Newham the design principle is about making the system work for learners, with the 'glue' of individual support being incorporated.

Programmes such as these tend to use open college or other accreditation rather than full level 2 vocational or the *Skills for Life* qualifications. They are therefore now vulnerable to cuts in 'other' further education funding and rely for their protection if any on the understanding and support of local Learning and Skills Councils:

> National pressures on 'other further education' mean that local LSCs will need to understand how credit-based qualifications contribute to achieving national targets, employer engagement and implementing equality and diversity policies. (Champney, Davey and Lawrence, 2005, p. 51)

The real significance of the new learning pathway proposal is now clear. It called for policy to be based on understanding the nature of learners' experiences and to enable curriculum development in response. Although this was not achieved, the political climate of 1997 and the context of the 1992 Further and Higher Education Act gave individual providers a good deal of freedom to innovate in the interests of widening participation, even if they were irked by the limitations of the funding methodology. But without the policy recognition, innovatory solutions on the lines of the pathway were marginal to what was left of the widening participation project. In the far more directive climate of the second and third terms of the Labour government, providers' ability to respond was more and more squeezed by the constraints of targets and funding, mediated through the planning role of the LSC. Paradoxically, the FEFC, which was not a planning body and as I have suggested was reluctant to take on a wider leadership role, did succeed in creating a positive context for widening participation, through not only the Kennedy report but the Tomlinson report on inclusive learning.

A further paradox lies in the way in which other elements of further education policy and other departments of government have been given or appropriated the space to innovate while the heart of the system is constrained. For example, a progressive first-term educational action was the recognition and encouragement of union learning representatives and the establishment of the Union Learning Fund, to be followed by Treasury commitment to investment in the TUC's Union Academy (DfES, 2005). The network of union learning representatives and the role of the unions tackle much the same agenda as the new learning pathway in a way which the Kennedy Committee did not anticipate. Or again, the first term Policy Action Teams advocated a flexible, holistic approach to widening participation and creating a learning culture in deprived communities (PATS, 1999). This can be followed through to work on learning for neighbourhood renewal (Office of the Deputy Prime Minister) and 'active learning for active communities' (Home Office), both of which recognise the diversity of learners' interests. It is telling that the LSC's widening participation strategy listed a much wider set of partners than did *Learning Works*, reflecting the social policy interest in learning in the early years of the Labour government (as well as the growing bureaucracy for skills). But it had no real programme for harnessing their efforts and inputs. While it would be foolish to deny the value of the creativity to be expected in initiatives outside mainstream further education, the polarisation against which McGivney warned in 1990 is very present.

There is a sharp contrast between the optimism created by the Kennedy Committee's confidence in the ability and willingness of institutions to deliver, and the tone of the report of the 2005 independent enquiry on the state of adult learning in further education colleges, *Eight in Ten* (NIACE, 2005)[5]. The challenges described by the enquiry are, depressingly, not very different from those of 1997:

> There are, perhaps, four main challenges which will need to be addressed at all levels. These are: developing incentives and motivation for adults to learn, integrating approaches to adult learning, improving the quality and variety of provision, and improving policy coherence and effectiveness. It may be that the fourth of these is the most crucial: it may also be the hardest to achieve. But it will not be possible to make real progress in the other areas without radical rethinking of policy about lifelong learning. (NIACE, 2005, p. 46)

But there is a striking change of mood, shown by the fieldwork, that the college sector's sense of itself and what its mission ought to be is now very different from the government's objectives and targets and that this undermines development:

> ...the need for college staff to reclaim a sense of agency and authority in curriculum and qualification design, delivery and assessment. (NIACE, 2005, p. ix)

A report of a four-year independent study into teaching in further education (*Transforming Learning Cultures in FE*) supports this point:

> We have strong evidence that tutors are hemmed in by targets, with a narrow set of definitions used to measure the quality of their work, and that this is stifling their energy and enthusiasm and also their performance. (Prof. David James quoted in Whittaker, 2005)

This essay has focused on further education colleges for three reasons. They were the subject of the Kennedy Report. More important, widening participation must address access to vocational learning because that matters to learners, with the provisos that accessible routes into vocational learning are of critical importance and that what is usually categorised as vocational learning may serve other purposes as well. And most important, because of the size of the sector and the level of spending on it: if learners are denied access to that, there is a denial of social justice.

But the issues affect adult and community learning services and voluntary providers as well. The areas of work which previously had FEFC funding (under the old 'schedule 2' of the 1992 Further and Higher Education Act) and continue to receive LSC funding on the same formula-funded basis as colleges now experience the same pressures. But other areas and providers have a stark choice: to develop formula-funded work according to national priorities for adult learning, or to stay within the area of 'learning for personal and community development', where the overall level of funding is safeguarded, but no more.

The problem is not just the difficulty of promoting curriculum change to widen participation in these circumstances. The division of esteem in further education between full qualifications in the National Framework and 'other further education' has a parallel in that between the rest of the system and unaccredited learning for personal development, which is demarcated in policy:

> There are millions of people in this country who pursue training and skills not for any job-related purpose, but for personal development, civic and social engagement, pleasure and interest . . . While the economic and vocational purposes of skills are vital, they are in no sense the whole story. (DfES, 2005, p. 55)

In the context of the White Paper this admission does not mean parity of esteem but rather reinforces a division of labour between the constituents of the LSC-funded sector, in which colleges are less likely to be able to fulfil broader social purposes and individuals will continue to have difficulty in making their way through the system for their own valid and possibly complex purposes. Arguably, although the creation of the Learning and Skills sector was intended to overset the organisational and funding barriers created by the 1992 Act and which Kennedy challenged, the impact of government policy has been to recreate these in other forms which cannot be in the interests of learners.

References

Champney, J., Davey, M. and Lawrence, S. (2005) *Breaking Down the Barriers: Success in Widening Participation – A Toolkit Approach*, London: LSDA

DfEE (1998) *Further Education in the Millennium: Response to the Kennedy Report*, London: DfEE

DfES (2005) *Skills: Getting on in Business, Getting on at Work*, London: TSO

FEFC (1996) *Inclusive Learning: Principles and Recommendations: a Summary of the Findings of the Learning Difficulties and/or Disabilities Committee*, Coventry: FEFC

FEFC (1997a) *Pathways to Success: the Widening Participation Committee Emerging Conclusions*, Coventry: FEFC

FEFC (1997b) *Consultation Document: The Widening Participation Committee*, Coventry: FEFC

FEFC (1997c) *How to Widen Participation: a Guide to Good Practice*, Coventry: FEFC

Kennedy, H. (1997) *Learning Works: Widening Participation in Further Education*, Coventry: FEFC

LSC (2003) *Successful Participation for All: Widening Adult Participation*, Coventry: LSC

LSC (2005) *Priorities for Success: Funding for Learning and Skills*, Coventry: LSC

McGivney, V. (1990) *Education's for Other People: Access to Education for Non-participant Adults*, Leicester: NIACE

NIACE (2005) *Eight in Ten: Adult Learners in Further Education: the Report of the Independent Committee of Enquiry Invited by the National Institute of Adult Continuing Education to Review the State of Adult Learning in Colleges of Further Education in England*, Leicester: NIACE

Parry, G. (2001) *Academic Snakes and Vocational Ladders: Fourth Philip Jones Memorial Lecture*, Leicester: NIACE

PATS (1999) *Skills for Neighbourhood Renewal: National Strategy Action Plan,* Social Exclusion Unit, Cabinet Office

Whittaker, M. (2005) 'Policy dithering hits teaching', *TES*, November 11, 2005

Notes

[1] Widening Participation Committee meeting to mark the first anniversary of the report's publication, 30 June 1998: personal note.
[2] Personal communication 10 July 1997
[3] Widening Participation Committee 30 June 1998 – unpublished.
[4] For 2005/06, NIACE estimates a loss of over 200,000 places (*Adults Learning*, 2005). The LSC intends a cut of £73 million in 2006/07 in provision for adults which is outside the National Qualifications Framework with an estimated net loss of 230,000 places (LSC, 2005). These losses directly affect provision aimed at widening participation.
[5] Interestingly, the report's presentation is similar to that of the Kennedy Report, using A5 (notoriously, the pocket or handbag size chosen by Helena Kennedy) – a tacit invitation to see it as a stock take?

Chapter 10

Adults in higher education – the search for a policy learning journey

Maria Slowey

The concept of the 'learning journey'

In 2003, Veronica McGivney undertook an in-depth study of winners of the NIACE Adult Learners' Week Awards. With her usual perspicuity in focusing on the hot issues of the day, she used this rich source of qualitative information to investigate the extent to which such a phenomenon as a 'typical' adult learning journey might actually exist and be revealed through this process. Her analysis showed:

> . . . individual learning routes of such complexity and diversity that it was impossible to find any consistent or typical patterns. Learning starting points varied enormously and most of the winners had moved in different directions through a range of (often unconnected) both accredited and non-accredited subjects at different levels. As well as moving sideways across different subject areas, many had also progressed to higher-level learning. This was characteristic of those seeking employment and those seeking satisfaction and life enrichment. (McGivney, 2003, p. 7)

McGivney's key conclusion that, while learning may well be cumulative, it is rarely a linear process, came as little surprise to either the research or practitioner communities. The learning trajectory of an individual at any particular point does of course build upon biography and previous experience. It is however subject to constant reshaping as a consequence of changing social, economic, cultural and personal circumstances.

It is all very well for individual learning journeys to follow the unexpected and serendipitous – but what happens when we shift the focus from the individual to the policy level? Given the significant public, voluntary and private collective effort involved in policy development, might it not be reasonable to expect to find some evidence of learning from policy memory? Should a study of the archaeology of a particular policy strand not reveal a learning journey which demonstrates some degree of cumulative development?

Over the past twenty years or so the UK, in common with other EU and OECD countries, has been subject to a plethora of policy initiatives in the various sectors which either directly or indirectly impinge on the learning of the adult population – ranging from community education through work-based learning to further education, higher education, NGO and private sector provision. For much of this period of time adult education or adult learning, has been increasingly subsumed within the broader policy arena of lifelong learning.

The politics of policy development in the large arena of post-compulsory education and training are fascinating matters which are well discussed elsewhere (for different dimensions see Barnett, 2003; Coffield, 2000; Field, 2000; Henkel, 2000; Parry and Thompson, 2002; Scott, 1995, 2002; Smith and Webster, 1997; Taylor, 2005; Tuckett, 2003). In this chapter my perspective is somewhat more personal. Over this period I have had the good fortune to work on matters relating to adult participation in education in four quite different contexts – as a research officer on a large scale project; as head of a local authority adult education centre in London; as head of a centre for continuing education in a polytechnic; and as head of a department of adult education in a research-intensive university. As something of an insider/outsider on the UK scene (from Ireland, but working in England and Scotland for many years) I decided to use elements of my own learning journey as a mechanism through which policy learning journeys might also be traced.

Any journey through the highways and byways of national policy themes and initiatives is inevitably going to be a selective one. This chapter does not aspire to present a comprehensive analysis of policy initiatives associated with adults in higher education since the mid 1980s. On the other hand, the national initiatives considered here are more than a random selection. In one way or another they were intended to build cumulatively on the experience and evidence established by former initiatives – to this extent, it would be hoped that they might go beyond the 'complexity and diversity' that

McGivney had identified for learning undertaken by individuals, drawing in a cumulative manner on knowledge and collective experience.

My particular focus is on a range of policy strands which carried potential implications for adult participation in higher education. This is not to suggest that this is by any means the largest or most significant topic meriting attention from the perspective of the learning interests of the adult population. It is simply that, as adult learning is so ubiquitous and varied in nature, for pragmatic reasons it is useful to focus on one particular dimension in order to make the selection manageable.

The reality behind the rather grand phrase 'policy engagement' can on occasion appear synonymous with participation in committee meetings (of the interminable variety), held on Friday afternoons (in rather inaccessible locations) with trains and plane schedules all in some turmoil (due to expected/unexpected bouts of frost, leaves on the lines etcetera, etcetera), all accompanied by wheel-barrows full of documentation. However these minor inconveniences are by far outweighed by the stimulation of working with colleagues who, coming from a wide range of perspectives (frequently conflicting) and structural positions demonstrate extraordinary commitment to seeking new ways of working through complex issues.

My exploration of these issues is organised into three parts:

The *first part* sets the context through reflections on the processes and outcomes of what remains the most comprehensive national survey of adults in education in England and Wales. This study was commissioned by the Department of Education and Science in the early 1980s. The emphasis placed on independent, rigorous, social research as a basis for the development of policy reflected an approach, which, to its great credit, has been actively promoted by NIACE over many decades.

The *second part* moves on to consideration of a number of major policy themes over a twenty-year period, with which I have been personally involved in England (in some cases acting as a proxy for British policy as a whole) and Scotland. Three criteria influenced this selection of policy themes and initiatives:

- First, despite building upon different terms of reference and objectives, all touch upon matters of potential relevance to adult learners in higher education.

138

- Second, the status of each of these policy initiatives is varied. Some are independent commissions set up by Government, while others are committees and groups working under the auspices of national funding and quality agencies.
- Third, the initiatives could be considered as being to some extent representative of 'their time', reflecting the broader social and economic context from which they emerged.

The *final part* returns again to consideration of the potential contribution of research to cumulative policy learning in relation to adult and continuing education.

The Mature Students Research Project: a benchmark

A quarter of a century ago what remains one of the most comprehensive surveys on adult learners in England and Wales was commissioned, after a competitive tendering process, by the Department of Education and Science. The successful research consortium comprised three institutions – the Open University, the Polytechnic of Central London and Lancaster University. The Mature Students Project was led by individuals who have made a remarkable contribution over many years to research and policy development relating to widening access to post-compulsory education by under-represented sections of the population – Oliver Fulton, Keith Percy, Naomi Sargant, Leslie Wagner and Alan Woodley. Applying for one of the research officer positions from Ireland, where I had been Research Fellow at AONTAS – the National Association of Adult Education – I had little idea at the time how fortunate this move would prove to be in terms of engagement with a project that would become something of a benchmark.

The detailed questionnaire developed by the Mature Students Research Project was returned by over five-and-a-half thousand adults engaged in structured learning of some significant kind across England and Wales. The sampling framework was sophisticated, allowing for weighting across different categories of respondents. On reflection now, the seven categories of learners identified for inclusion at the time carry a certain 'historical' feel. Students were sampled on the basis of attendance at courses within the following categories:

a) Courses ranging from three-year tutorials to one-year or two-year part-time courses.

b) Open University courses.
c) Day release or block release (including part-time further education courses of a substantial nature).
d) Extended 'fresh horizons or new opportunities' courses.
e) Part-time 'internal' degree and other advanced courses in higher education establishments, including universities.
f) Correspondence courses of at least two terms' duration.
g) Courses at long-term residential colleges.

The analysis focused mainly on motivational issues and barriers to engagement in learning in post-initial education. The categories above might well appear somewhat dated in an era when the terminology has significantly shifted from adult education to lifelong learning and when, for example, it is only the very interested, historians and tutors and students – of a rather mature vintage – who are likely to recall what a 'tutorial class' was!

Despite the quite different social political and economic circumstances pertaining today however, it is interesting to reflect on the extent to which a number, possibly most, of the conclusions remain relevant. For example:

> For part-time students, the financial problem is the fees incurred in enrolling in a course. This is most likely to affect two major under-represented groups – women and working-class students. The NAB [National Advisory Board for Public Sector Higher Education] report's recommendation that part-time fees should be reduced seems both timely and appropriate, particularly for those groups at present under-represented. It is in this area that a small amount of money is likely to go a long way in stimulating greater participation. (Woodley *et al*, 1987, p. 177)

The above observations particularly related to students taking courses leading to some form of certification in universities, other higher education institutions or further education colleges. The research had demonstrated a statistically significant distinction at the time in terms of educational background and motivation between those students who embarked on a programme leading to qualifications and those on what were termed 'non-qualifying courses'. In the latter case, in a pre-lifelong learning era, the analysis points to the fact that learners engaged in courses not directly leading to a qualification had 'experienced sharp rises in fees in the years prior to our survey'.

> In the hard times in which we are now supposed to live, the 'indulgence of leisure' courses must, it is said, be paid for. We find this view neither equitable nor persuasive – nor yet adequate as a description of such courses. (Woodley *et al*, 1987, p. 177)

The extensive investigation of adults in different forms of structured education concluded with a recognition of their perseverance and dedication. While acknowledgement is given to the innovative work undertaken by institutions,

> . . . we cannot escape the feeling that collectively educational institutions exhibit a fairly high degree of caution in their attitude to mature students. (Woodley *et al*, 1987, p. 179)

I have no doubt about the nature of the personal learning journey which I experienced in the course of the conduct of the Mature Students Project. But what about the policy learning journey? The Mature Students Project was conducted and reported upon in the turmoil of the early period of Thatcherism which challenged many fundamental concepts, not least the very existence of society itself. While it would be interesting to trace the policy continuity or otherwise with the early phases of neo-liberalism some twenty or so years later, the question addressed in this chapter is rather different.

The barriers to adults learning in higher education were well, and repeatedly, identified over this period – resulting from a complex interaction of factors such as social class, previous educational experience and gender with the structural, economic and socio-cultural nature of higher education provision (for example, McGivney, 1990, 1996). Given the existence of this body of knowledge about barriers to participation, the issue that fascinated me was the extent to which it might be possible to trace a 'policy journey' which may have led to these barriers being addressed, and possibly reduced, in any significant way.

Adults in higher education: a 25-year policy-learning journey?

This 25-year period of higher education was characterised by a dramatic expansion in terms of student numbers. Total numbers almost doubled between 1985 and 2001, including a major increase – in both absolute and relative terms – of women, mature students and post-graduates, with less clear evidence on social class profiles, part-time undergraduates outside the Open University, students with disabilities and other groups (Slowey and Watson, 2003). This expansion was accompanied by numerous policy initiatives aimed at steering the system which, directly or indirectly, carried implications for adult learners.

Policy themes are rarely discrete in terms of origin, focus, impact or chronology. The extent to which the five identified in Table 9.1 are amongst the most significant in relation to adults in higher education is, of course, open to debate. Another selection might, for example, certainly have included *widening access*, *continuing professional development* and *lifelong learning*. However, as the latter are well covered in current literature I regarded this an opportunity to highlight some different themes which, it seemed to me, should also feature on any league table over the period in question.

The associated initiatives discussed here are examples, selected from many, to illustrate the ways in which larger policy themes have been operationalised. In each case I had the opportunity to view developments from both sides, that is from the perspective of someone engaged with a national initiative (through committee involvement and the like), as well as operating at the institutional level – the object in most cases of these initiatives. Reflecting on my own geographical wanderings, I have also drawn from developments originating both north and south of Hadrian's Wall.

Table 9.1 Schematic timeline, selected policy themes and initiatives

Period	Theme	Illustrative initiative
1980s		
	(i) Credit accumulation	Council for National Academic Awards (CNAA)
	(ii) Equal opportunities	National Advisory Body (NAB)
1990s–2000+		
	(iii) Quality	Higher Education Quality Council (HEQC)
	(iv) Research	Research Assessment Exercise (RAE)
	(v) Funding	*Cubie* Committee

The 1980s: credit accumulation and transfer and equal opportunities

(i) Credit accumulation and transfer

In 1984 the bodies responsible for the two higher education sectors, NAB (National Advisory Body for Public Sector Education) and UGC (University Grants Committee) both published reports on continuing education.

Much of the debate at the time was influenced directly or indirectly by a momentum developed under the auspices of the Council for National Academic Awards (CNAA). From around the mid-1980s the CNAA had promulgated the notion of credit accumulation and transfer as a key mechanism in the introduction of flexibility and widening access for mature students with work and previous life experiences into higher education.

These developments were promoted through the work of the CNAA CATS (Credit Accumulation and Transfer Scheme Committee) especially over the period 1987 to 1992 (see for example, CNAA, 1989). It could be – and was at the time – argued that the thinking which underlay the NAB and UGC reports on continuing education and CATS developments represented something of a paradigm shift. The focus of attention was to move *from* the provider *to* the learner – taking account of their diversity of backgrounds, motivations, interests and educational needs. The emphasis was on flexibility and choice in terms of both mode of provision (part-time, full-time, distance) and the curriculum.

The ultimate vision was of individual learning pathways, encompassing the assessment of prior learning developed in both formal and non-formal contexts.

My personal reflection of being a member of the CNAA CATS Committee is something of a seesaw experience. The 'highs' were generated by discussions of approaches and principles more traditionally associated with the adult education community featuring prominently in discussions about the future shape of higher education. These were however counterbalanced by the 'lows' associated with rather esoteric debates about the nature of credit and the extent to which the student workload over an academic year should constitute 30, 60, 90 or any other number of credits. At another level, the discussion focused on the extent to which greater flexibility and student choice was a 'good thing' or was simply moving towards treating students as consumers, thereby fuelling the free market ideology of Thatcherism.

There was also a nagging doubt about how real the opportunities might become, given the scale of institutional change involved, and how many adult learners actually wanted to, or could, avail of them. With a number of notable exceptions (such as Middlesex, Paisley, Northumbria, Sheffield Hallam) the primary interest of the higher education sector proved to be more associated with curricula and organisational matters relating to modularity, as opposed to promoting flexibility for adults and part-time learners (for example, Watson, 1989). This administrative legacy can be seen today as the Higher Education Funding Councils consider basing funding models on credits (HEFCE, 2005) and the European Credit Transfer Scheme is used to underpin the Bologna process.

(ii) Equal opportunities

A rather different starting point provides the base on which the equality of opportunity movement of the 1980s emerged. In relation to higher education, a major report was published under the auspices of NAB (1988). The strength of this report lay in its attempt to take a comprehensive and integrated approach to considerations of equity and access in higher education. The interests of mature students and part-time students were thus located within a considerably broader context.

> In general part-time students receive no support from public funds to cover the cost of studying in higher education. This is an issue of the greatest concern as it is this mode of study that frequently suits many 'non-traditional' entrants. Transport, books, childcare and similar additional costs which arise from participation in higher education are likely to be a burden for these groups of students. (NAB, 1988, p. 49)

This report did also consider CAT schemes and their potential support for particular target groups of students concluding that the '. . . development of these innovations is very patchy' and that a great deal of the resources provided to support innovations in these areas were only available on a short-term pump priming basis (NAB, 1988, p. 57). To a considerable extent the strength of the 1988 *Action for Access* report was also probably a weakness as its comprehensive focus posed a challenge to both policy makers and institutions.

The attempt to address access and equity issues in this integrated way was in any case overtaken by events as the main energy of the higher education systems was devoted – or arguably diverted – to the establishment of a unified system bringing together the institutions, the polytechnic sector, with the previously existing university sector.

The 1990s–present: quality, research and funding

In reflecting on the 1990s, while issues of access and equity for adult and part-time students did crop up from time to time as part of the higher education policy context, arguably the dominant agenda was driven by three other concerns underpinning the new 'mass' system – quality, research and funding. These themes were so dominant that, despite the political change that took place over the decade from a Conservative to a Labour Government, a considerable degree of continuity is apparent in the policy agenda.

(iii) The quality industry

The strengthening of the audit culture was one of the defining features of this period.

In terms of adult learner interests, on the plus side, the quality agenda did point to issues relating to the learning needs of different categories of students. Through the work of the HEQC for example, development work continued in relation to credit accumulation and transfer schemes under the auspices of the HEQC Credit and Access Advisory Group. In 1994, this Group produced a major report *Choosing to Change: Extending Access, Choice and Mobility in Higher Education*. This report reviewed developments to that point in terms of institutional and sectoral change. While highlighting areas of innovation, the overall conclusion however was that progress could be described as little better than patchy.

> Our investigations suggest that there is indeed considerable scepticism within all universities, but particularly within the older institutions, towards the rationale for the introduction of modular and credit-based systems. Too frequently, it is perceived as an attempt to increase the productivity of universities and materially deteriorate the conditions of professional life at a time when policy towards the sector is generally so perceived. (HEQC, 1994, p. 70)

More generally, under the various forms of Teaching Assessment conducted by the Higher Education Funding Councils, addressing the needs of mature students did become a matter to be highlighted for consideration in self-assessment documents and peer review visits. In my own institution at the time, the University of Glasgow, colleagues in the Department of Adult and Continuing Education (DACE) found it rather gratifying when subject departments undergoing an assessment exercise requested engagement by DACE part-time adult learners in order to demonstrate their commitment to widening access.

On the other hand, the rigidities and paper-driven approaches that charac-terised some aspects of this system at certain periods of the 1990s has been subject to widespread critique. Morley, for example, in her empirical study of power and quality in universities reports that '. . . no informant actually cited improved teaching or enhanced disciplinary knowledge as outcomes of quality assessment. They all tended to focus on procedures, structures and documentation' (Morley, 2003, p. 85).

(iv) Research

The emphasis on quality and quantity of research output from British universities undoubtedly accelerated from the 1992, through to the 1996 and 2001 Research Assessment Exercises (RAE) conducted by the Higher Education Funding Councils for England, Scotland and Wales. An important factor underlying this focus was a perceived need for UK research – and the elite universities in particular – to become better positioned in a globally competitive environment.

This may seem a long way from our interest in this chapter in adult and part-time learners. Does it matter if research is increasingly concentrated in a small number of centres of excellence? Or, if something akin to a transfer market exists for high-flying research 'stars'? Or, if academic departments – even institutions – merge and reorganise with a view to better positioning in terms of research environment, support for research students and the like?

In this, as in other areas touched upon in this chapter, an expert body of work exists investigating the impact of the RAE from a variety of perspectives. Drawing on this more formal analysis, my own reflections are also shaped by my experiences both sides of the fence – as a member of the RAE Continuing Education Sub-Panel in both 1996 and 2001, and as Head of a Department of

Adult and Continuing Education in a research–intensive university for much of that period.

On the positive side, it has to be hoped that the outcome of this enormous effort ultimately will be to deliver better quality research concerning adult students and higher education from sociological, psychological, educational and economic perspectives. It seems to me however, there are two areas in which the dynamics of the RAE may ultimately have a profound impact on the nature of educational opportunities available to adults in higher education.

Firstly, for a variety of reasons the status of research has increased markedly as a consequence of the RAE exercise. The reasons are indeed complex as the direct resource rewards, while important, may not be very significant in monetary terms as a percentage of overall institutional budgets outside the small number of highly research-intensive institutions. Undoubtedly, achievement of a high grade is important in reputational terms and hence in securing resources from other sources. However, for many departments in many universities achieving a relatively average grade, it is not always easy to see how the reward might be proportional to the effort invested.

The differentiation in status associated with RAE gradings operates both between institutions and within institutions. Despite an emphasis in the RAE criteria on dissemination of research findings and links between practitioners and user groups, there is a widely perceived tension between delivery of the research agenda on the one hand, and teaching new groups of learners and building connections with the world of work and the broader community on the other.

At a national level, leaving aside the Open University and some specialist institutions, widening access tends to be associated with non-elite universities (Siner and Modood, 2002) while high research rankings are associated to a considerable extent with elite, older universities (McNay, 2003). This is hardly news. It does mean however, that previous patterns continue to be reinforced. The status distinction also operates within institutions. Anecdotally, colleagues from a number of institutions have suggested that some of the worst tempered committee debates in their respective universities tend to be in the research areas with suggestions of strong egos bruising against each other and rather 'macho' styles of interaction on display regardless of the gender of the individuals involved.

Secondly, the RAE has an effect at the departmental level as academic staff in many institutions see their career pathways associated with research and publication, leaving even the most dedicated of teachers with competing demands on their time. There has been an additional, specific impact on university departments of education, adult education and their like in particular, which, in different ways over many decades, had a tradition of delivery of programmes for adult learners underpinned by research. This issue is highlighted by the Director of the ESRC Teaching and Learning Research Programme – the largest scale educational research initiative, conducted in the UK – in his review of the state of educational research:

> ...there is a significant and growing amount of high quality education and educational work in the UK, both qualitative and quantitative. This draws on social scientific designs and methods and is gradually building a more sophisticated understanding of enduring educational issues. However, such work is undertaken by only a minority of educationalists in HE, with a concentration in research-intensive universities (Pollard, 2005, p. 12)

In the case of the Department of Adult and Continuing Education at the University of Glasgow we developed a research strategy which built explicitly on our connection with the field of practice, in terms of adults in higher education, community education, work-based learning and the like. We were fortunate in that this strategy, although not easy to deliver, proved sustainable. This however has not been the experience of many other excellent university adult/continuing education units, centres or departments with expertise in both delivery and research, which have been buffeted, in some cases to the point of fragmentation, by the impact of different funding streams.

(v) Funding

The major focus on research and research ranking undoubtedly impacted on the structure of the higher education system at national levels and internally. However, in terms of profile outside the education policy communities, it is the question of *student funding* which attracted the most public attention over the 1990s and into the twenty-first century. For England and Wales, the National Committee of Inquiry into Higher Education, chaired by Sir Ron Dearing, was the most comprehensive review undertaken since the Robbin's Review of Higher Education in 1963. While the Dearing Report did address issues of equity, access, lifelong learning and the like, the attention of the main stakeholders – Government, the public, employers and institutions – was on the question of funding mechanisms for full-time students, and essentially associated with those directly progressing from initial education in schools and colleges.

The scale of the National Commission exercise was so enormous that at the time a fly-on-the-wall observer would be forgiven for wondering who was left teaching, undertaking research and running institutions as so many of us participated in committees, working groups and consultative exercises of one kind or another. The processes and impact of its work has been the subject of extensive detailed analysis, including from a lifelong learning perspective (Watson and Taylor, 1998). One way or the other, implementation of recommendations from the point of view of adults and part-time learners proved disappointing to say the least.

The funding theme continued to occupy higher education policy debates in the latter part of the 1990s as the constitutional changes associated with the devolution of Scotland and, subsequently Wales, independently addressed the question of student finance in higher education. (For anyone with a general interest in the contexts and implications of devolution the ESRC Devolution Programme provides a mine of interesting material.)

The first action of the Scottish Parliament in 1999 was to set up an Independent Committee of Inquiry into Student Finance, chaired by Andrew Cubie. In terms of personal learning journeys, this does stand out for me as being of particular significance – at one level there was the excitement of working with the devolved structures, exploring the boundaries as to what was possible within the new constitutional framework. At another level there was the intensity of the process as the Committee was given a five-month timescale in which to submit its report. The process adopted placed a significant emphasis on consultation with the pubic, in addition to extensive discussions with a wide variety of the major stakeholders. Thirteen public hearings were held throughout Scotland and more than seven hundred individual and organisational submissions were received.

Included under the Guiding Principles set out by the Committee, was the objective that the Government should remove barriers to widening access and participation by:

- targeting resources effectively on sections of society under-represented in both further and higher education programmes;
- providing flexible means of support to accommodate the changing nature of the student population;
- assisting, in particular, those students who may not otherwise obtain sufficient support so that education is available to all those with the ability to benefit from study. (Independent Committee, 1997, p.17).

While the major focus of the Report was on issues relating to the level and nature of the financing of full-time studies, Chapter 5 explicitly evaluated and addressed support for part-time students, including those in further education, those in higher education and those on non-credit bearing courses. The Report also addressed the challenges facing mature students in further and higher education. Several stakeholder organisations including, for example, the University Association for Continuing Education, the Committee of Scottish Higher Education Principals, the National Union of Students and the Open University – had indeed lobbied on behalf of part-time students, making a case that they should, at a minimum, be supported pro-rata to full-time students.

However, analysis of the issues raised at the public discussions and in the majority of submissions received revealed what could only be described as a public, political and organisational *silence* in relation to the issues and challenges facing part-time learners. This was in total contrast to the evidence of extensive public and political debate and lobbying associated with access to higher education by school-leavers – and it is not surprising therefore that it is the latter voice which tends to get heard.

Conclusion: The search for a policy learning journey. A triumph of optimism over experience?

The concept of 'evidence based' policy is one which has gained a considerable degree of currency in recent years. The attractions of developing policy based on analysis of 'what works' as opposed to personal bias, hunches, dominant vested interests and the like, are apparent. There is a clear connection here with the notion of the policy learning journey of cumulative learning, from research and evaluation of outcomes as we experiment, evaluate, refine and develop. The reality of course is far more complex. To highlight just three out of many factors: the critical impact of power dynamics in the commissioning, selection, profiling and interpretation of research (for example, Kogan, 2005); the ambiguous nature not to mention quality of much research undertaken; the fact that the – by definition – empiricist, policy imperative to seek to discover 'what works' is problematic in itself.

Despite these challenges and constraints a key question remains: is there anything better on offer? The reflections outlined in this chapter lead me towards the conclusion that it is important to 'keep on plugging'. Independent rigorous research which has a direct impact on policy and policy development which forms a learning journey may be the exception rather than the rule. However, progress can be discerned in some areas.

One particular group of adult learners, namely part-time students in higher education, have in one way or another cropped up across the policy initiatives considered here – sometimes as a category, a challenge, a vacuum and, not infrequently, as a problem. It is too early to judge, however the recent announcement by HEFCE appears to be giving a new profile, not to mention some resources, to supporting part-time opportunities in higher education. There are hundreds of thousands of adults who might wish to pursue higher education study, but who want to stay engaged in work, domestic duties and the like and are not in a position to and/or may not want to, become 'full-time' students with all that implies. Might this new initiative represent a turning point?

The level of funding involved is probably equivalent to investment in a couple of university sports complexes. However, to the extent that adults in general, and part-time learners in particular, feature on the policy agenda at all, reflects to some extent a response to the consistent lobbying and investigation of these issues over long periods of time by dedicated individuals and organisations.

To borrow Woodley's phrase, if at long last it might be an 'amber light' for part-timers in higher education, then this may indeed suggest some evidence of the existence of a policy learning journey (Woodley, 2004). Optimism however must be tempered by experience as, despite decades of exploration of the potential social, economic and personal benefits of shifting from a front-loaded education system, policy and resourcing remains focused on extending initial education (schooling) for young people as opposed to supporting the learning needs of a broader population through recurrent education (in 1970s terminology) continuing education (1980s) or lifelong learning (1990s).

References

Barnett, R. (2003) *Beyond All Reason: Living with Ideology in the University*, Buckingham: SRHE/Open University Press

Coffield, F. (Ed.) (2000) *Differing Visions of a Learning Society*, Bristol: Policy Press

CNAA (1989) *Credits for Change: The CNNA Credit Accumulation and Transfer Scheme and the Universities*, London: CNNA

Field, J. (2000) *Lifelong Learning and the New Educational Order*, London: Trentham Books

Henkel, M. (2000) *Academic Identities and Policy Change in Higher Education*, London: Jessica Kingsley

HEFCE (2005) *£40 Million Boost for Part-Time Students*, available at http://www.hefce.ac.uk/news/hefce/2005/ptboost.htm

HEQC (1994) *Choosing to Change: Extending Access, Choice and Mobility in Higher Education*, (The Robertson Report), London: HEQC

Independent Committee of Inquiry into Student Finance (1999) *Student Finance: Fairness for the Future* (*The Cubie Report*), Edinburgh: Independent Committee of Inquiry into Student Finance)

Kogan, M. (2005) 'Modes of knowledge and patterns of power', *Higher Education*, 49(102): 9–30

McGivney, V. (1990) *Education's for Other People*, Leicester: NIACE

McGivney, V. (1996) *Staying or Leaving the Course*, Leicester: NIACE

McGivney, V. (2003) *Adult learning pathways: through routes or cul de sacs?*, Leicester: NIACE

NcNay, I. (2003) 'Assessing the assessment: an analysis of the UK research assessment Exercise 2001, and its outcomes, with special reference to research in education', *Science and Public Policy*, 30(91): 1–8

Morley, L. (2003) 'Reconstructing students as consumers: power and assimilation?' in M. Slowey and D. Watson (eds) *Higher Education and the Lifecourse*, Maidenhead: SRHE/Open University Press

National Advisory Body for Public Sector Higher Education (1984) *Report of the Continuing Education Group*, London: NAB

National Advisory Body for Public Sector Higher Education (1988) *Action for Access: Widening Opportunities in Higher Education*, London: NAB

National Committee on Inquiry into Higher Education (1997) *Higher Education in the Learning Society* (*The Dearing Report*), London: HMSO

Parry, G. and Thompson, A. (2002) *Closer by Degrees: The Past, Present and Future of Higher Education in Further Education Colleges*, London: LSDA

Pollard, A. (2005) *Taking the Initiative? TLRP and Education Research*, paper presented at the *Educational Review* Guest Lecture, University of Birmingham, October

Scott, P. (1995) *The Meaning of Mass Higher Education*, Buckingham: SRHE/Open University Press

Scott, P. (2002) *HE: An Overview*, Leicester: Universities Association for Continuing Education (UACE) Occasional Paper 26

Shiner, M. and Modood, T. (2002) Help or Hindrance? Higher Education and the Road to Ethnic Equality, *British Journal of Sociology of Education*, 23(2): 209–32

Slowey, M. and Watson, D. (eds) (2003) *Higher Education and the Lifecourse*, Maidenhead: SRHE/Open University Press

Smith, A. and Webster, F. (eds) (1997) *The Post-Modern University? Contested Visions of Higher Education in Society*, Buckingham: SRHE/Open University Press

Taylor, R. (2005) 'Lifelong Learning Policy and the Labour Governments 1997–2004', *Oxford Review of Education*, 31(1): 101–118

Watson, D. and Taylor, R. (1998) *Lifelong Learning and the University: a Post-Dearing Agenda*, London: Falmer Press

Tuckett, A. (2003?) (Note: to find ref for Leeds lecture)

University Grants Committee (1984) *Report of the Continuing Education Working Group*, London: UGC

Watson, D. (1989) *Managing the Modular Course*, Milton Keynes: Open University Press

Woodley, A., Wagner, L., Slowey, M., Hamilton, M., Fulton, O. (1987) *Choosing to Learn: Adults in Education*, Milton Keynes: SRHE/Open University Press

Woodley, A. (2004) *Earning, Learning and Paying: The Results from a National Survey of the Costs and Financing of Part-Time Students in Higher Education*, Buckingham: Open University

Chapter 11

Learning society, relations of learning: civic engagement and widening participation in the work of Veronica McGivney

John Field

All serious studies of participation in adult learning must start by reckoning with Veronica McGivney. Her work provides an essential empirical baseline for UK researchers in this large and academically mature field of inquiries, and her concern for equity and social justice is widely shared by researchers studying widening participation. Her influence reaches far beyond a particular national context, and equally McGivney herself has often drawn on international research to inform her own investigations of the UK. Participation studies are one of the hallmarks of adult education research internationally, and it is also an area where scholarly interests overlap with the priorities of many practitioners and sympathetic policymakers. McGivney's prominence, and the nature of her contribution, deserve serious – and critical – attention.

In this chapter, I follow up one of McGivney's many insights into adult participation in learning. In a number of key studies, McGivney has first postulated and subsequently explored the existence of a connection between active citizenship and participation in learning. She suggested the likelihood of such a relationship in her synthesis of studies of participation, *Education's for Other People* (McGivney, 1990, pp. 12–13), and subsequently returned to it in later work. This chapter sets McGivney's contribution into the context of contemporary British scholarship in adult participation, before going on to explore McGivney's own attention to active citizenship and adult learning.

It then reviews more recent research into this topic, which has tended both to confirm McGivney's original insights into the existence of a connection between the two while also developing a more complex and nuanced understanding of the nature and potential of that relationship.

Researching participation

McGivney's influence on participation research has been an enduring one. Her seminal synthesis (McGivney, 1990) has been particularly widely cited, and was adopted as a core text on a number of graduate courses. It may be helpful to reflect briefly on how this came about, not least because it helps us see just how profound a change McGivney helped bring about. Participation has long been a central topic for adult education researchers, in part because – in these islands as elsewhere – many of the investigators were also practitioners or managers, who carried out their studies with one eye to a better understanding of student recruitment. Yet until well into the 1980s, much of the conceptual framework, together with the methodology, derived from a number of influential North American studies. As well as the pioneering, if somewhat eclectic work of Cyril Houle, scholars such as Patricia Cross, Sean Courtney and Gordon Darkenwald had sought to identify the typical characteristics of adult learners, usually with a view to developing a typology of typical learner groups.

While the North American studies dominated the theoretical and methodological landscape, there was also an important local British tradition of empirically grounded participation research. In particular, McGivney's own employer, the National Institute of Adult Continuing Education and its predecessor body (the National Institute of Adult Education), has conducted a series of large-scale cross-sectional surveys of the adult population, focusing on the patterns and characteristics of participation. The first NIAE survey, conducted in 1969, found that people studying in courses offered by a local authority or university/Workers Educational Association were far more likely than non-students to belong to clubs or societies, and to take an active interest in community service and cultural pursuits (NIAE, 1970, pp. 145–8). Government agencies have also promoted such surveys; the Advisory Council for Adult and Continuing Education (ACACE), created by the Labour Government of James Callaghan, commissioned a national survey in the early 1980s. More recently the Department for Education and Skills has commissioned its own adult learning surveys. These studies are widely known and continue to be frequently cited by scholars within the UK.

They have been particularly important in drawing attention to systematic inequalities of participation, such as those associated with socio-economic status, age, gender and perhaps above all, level of schooling. Although they have sometimes been criticised for overemphasising formal adult education and training, and thus downplaying or ignoring informal learning, in recent years NIACE and DfES surveys have made increasingly sophisticated attempts to investigate self-directed learning and other less formal types of adult learning.

This important body of work has served as a platform for a highly developed approach to the empirical study of participation. However, as in much other adult education research, the large-scale surveys were accompanied by a considerable number of studies that were comparatively small scale, local and practise-based, with few attempts to engage critically with the wider literature on participation. Dick Taylor and I argued in the mid-1990s that the field of adult education research had till then tended to be dominated numerically by a large volume of one-off studies, often undertaken by practitioners (including university lecturers in extra-mural departments) as part of a higher degree (Field and Taylor, 1995). Until the early 1990s, systematic reviews of the literature, and sustained conceptual or methodological debates, were either absent altogether, or were largely derived from developments in other, usually more abstract and less professionally relevant disciplines.

During the 1980s and 1990s, though, research into adult learning changed in a number of significant ways. Partly, this was due to a wider conceptual and linguistic shift in the way that the field of practice has been analysed and described, a process that both expressed and reflected a shift of attention towards learning rather than education, and that allowed for – indeed, demanded – a closer alignment of researchers from our field with scholars from other social science disciplines. This shift has been discussed elsewhere, and is rightly seen as part of a wider set of social, economic, technological and cultural changes in contemporary Western societies (Edwards, 1997; Ranson, 1998; Field, 2006a). While these wider socio-economic changes continue to reshape the research agenda as well as provision and policy, they also made themselves felt through a series of relatively short-term consequences for the field, including the significant challenges presented by the rapid deindustrialisation of many manufacturing and extractive economies in the 1970s and early 1980s.

The 1970s had started as a period of optimism for adult education movements. Radical social movements in the West, particularly feminism, were often closely associated with adult education institutions whose origins lay in workers' education; in developing nations, national liberation movements – and sometimes the governments they generated – often promoted popular education. In Europe and elsewhere, Social Democratic and Christian Democratic governments were considering the merits of policies promoting lifelong education or recurrent education (these terms, though widely debated later on, were often used more or less interchangeably at the time). In Britain, for instance, these ideas led to government committees on adult education in both England and Scotland, as well as to the creation of the Advisory Council on Adult and Continuing Education, the foundation of a national agency for adult literacy, and the opening of a new residential adult college in South Yorkshire. But at the same time as raising the profile of adult learning, these developments often brought uncomfortable challenges for existing adult education institutions. NIACE, for example, was deeply unsettled by the fledgling literacy agency nesting in its premises; the worlds of workers' education and university extra-mural studies were riven by painful conflicts.

In the early 1970s, developments still promised a future of radical change and growth. By the mid-1970s, though, things had changed. Initially shaken by a relatively short-lived oil crisis, the long post-War economic boom collapsed across much of the West. The early onset of modern globalising tendencies also had a significant impact on the competitive position of Western manufacturing, particularly in such state-owned industries as steel, coal and car building. The collapse of well-established industries brought a new constituency into adult education, as governments sought to identify easily affordable practical solutions to the sudden appearance of mass unemployment. Few existing providers had significant experience with students – often male, middle aged, and very experienced craft workers – from backgrounds in manual work. Equally, conventional adult education was not part of the lifeworld of many of the newly unemployed. Relatively large mainstream institutions, such as Britain's further education colleges – previously concerned mainly with vocational and general provision for youth – were increasingly expected to attract adults, particularly the unemployed. At the same time, governments started to question and sometimes refocus or even redirect their existing investments in adult education. This was a very significant set of shifts, and inevitably change in the field generated new interests in research.

In particular, the sharp rise of mass adult unemployment brought about a reshaping of participation research. Until the early 1980s, most participation studies rested on the assumption that adult learners were essentially willing volunteers. In the new situation, providers were starting to identify 'target groups' who were not typical of the voluntary learners, and therefore had to be recruited by quite different techniques. Researchers, themselves often drawn from or active in the field, were inevitably affected by these changes. In particular, there was a new attention to what were often characterised as 'non-participant' groups – segments of the adult population who rarely featured in the dominant forms of adult education, but were now increasingly viewed as priorities for recruitment. Much applied research was inspired by the practical difficulties involved in this transformation of the field, some of it funded and even published by REPLAN, the national agency for developing education for the adult unemployed. McGivney and Sims's substantial overview study, although associated with REPLAN, was also aimed at a wider audience (McGivney and Sims, 1986).

Of course, this emerging body of work drew on, and benefited from, an earlier tradition of research into adult learning and socio-economic disadvantage. Three groups of scholars in particular were influential; those who had published (and usually worked) in the fields of trade union studies, women's studies and community education. Like those who wrote about adult education and the unemployed, these groups of scholars were deeply involved in the field of practice as well as scholarship, and they frequently shared passionately held views about the wider social purpose of their work. Typically, they also took the view that the link between adult learning and social commitment was close and immediate. Jane Thompson and other feminist adult education scholars, for example, drew inspiration from the women's movement, and also saw it as intrinsically a learning movement (Thompson, 1983). R.H. Tawney's dictum, to the effect that all social movements were also educational movements, was explored by socially committed adult educators in a book edited by the UK's leading community education scholar, with chapters by scholars deeply involved in social movement types of adult education (Lovett, 1988). These engaged scholars were certainly interested in who participated in adult learning, as well as in extending new opportunities to working-class people, women and/or members of disadvantaged communities. However, they tended to focus their attention on participation by members of the group that they happened to be interested in, and to attribute non-participation largely to the intentions of members of an oppressor group. In this respect, the individual accounts tended to over-simplify the issue of participation rather than problematising it, but collectively they strengthened the case for a systematic analysis of which adults were able to enter which types of education, while also drawing attention to the importance of social movements as a learning resource.

Finally, participation research was further stimulated by emerging policy debates over persistent inequalities in access to higher education. Again, this concern was relatively narrow, and usually linked to advocacy on behalf of the claims of a particular group – working class people, mature students, women and/or minority ethnic groups – to receive targeted supports. With relatively few exceptions, the access movement from the late 1970s and right through the 1980s was primarily concerned with one stage in the student life cycle – namely, the process of entry or recruitment into a higher education programme. It rarely addressed issues of continuing participation or of eventual outcomes, and with few exceptions researchers associated with the access movement showed little interest in civic engagement. Until Roseanne Benn examined this issue in the 1990s (Benn, 1996, 2000) researchers interested in access to higher education did not consider the dimension of civic engagement.

The importance of McGivney's contribution can only be grasped against this wider social, economic and above all intellectual background. In the short term, her influence was undoubtedly due in part to the extraordinary impact of *Education's for Other People* (McGivney, 1990), a text which significantly influenced the way that a large number of scholars and scholar-practitioners thought about adult education research, and more broadly has been used and cited repeatedly by a massive range of scholars and practitioners in the UK and beyond, becoming a standard text in taught post-graduate courses in adult learning. Extraordinarily for its time, it combined an attempt to take a learners' perspective with a systematic review of existing scholarship and research; relevance and rigour were not, it seemed, as incompatible as I at least had supposed.[1]

Participation and active citizenship in recent research

In *Education's for Other People*, McGivney argued that a number of factors should be considered in explaining participation and non-participation. She did not assume that either participation or non-participation were natural and obvious things for people to do, and she challenged any tendency to adopt a simplistic or mono-causal explanation. As one of a number of factors which might help explain participation in adult learning, McGivney drew attention to the role of civic engagement as a dimension that had previously been largely neglected, or at best simply asserted as though evidence was not required. This rather neatly exemplifies her scepticism over mono-causal explanations of participation; the point of examining civic engagement, she suggested, was that it could help explain variations within particular socio-economic groupings, such as the working class. While she certainly did not discount class as a factor she challenged her readers to see it as complex and overlaid with other factors, some structural and others more subjective or dispositional.

McGivney's emphasis on civic engagement as an independent factor was not entirely original, as we shall see. But it was made with some clarity, and was backed with reference to evidence. Moreover, in so far as this topic has been considered by others at all, most previous studies had tended to dwell on the impact of adult learning on civic engagement. Mainstream studies had tended to emphasise the value of adult education in fostering active and democratic participation, for example in trade unions or in local government, sometimes bolstering this argument with empirical evidence linking participation in learning and active citizenship (Groombridge *et al*, 1982). More radical writers argued that adult education could, and should, promote social action for fundamental change (Thompson, 1983); but most authors in the radical tradition tended to argue largely on ethical or political grounds, rather than from an empirical base.

McGivney's analysis contrasted with both approaches, though her work was certainly grounded on empirical research. Her concern lay in explaining participation in adult learning, with a particular focus on identifying those practices that might be adopted in order to widen participation to groups who were not traditionally part of the social milieu of adult education. Like much of McGivney's work, *Education's for Other People* drew on and synthesised the work of other researchers. In the case of civic engagement, McGivney drew above all on the work of the sociologist Jacques Hédoux, one of a team of French scholars who were then researching the everyday life of the working class. Led by Claude Dubar, one of France's most eminent sociologists and a specialist in studies of occupational identity, this group conducted a number of highly detailed studies of the social life of mining communities in northern France (Dubar, Gayot and Hédoux, 1982).

In his own work on the northern French mining communities in the 1970s, Hédoux had found that working-class adults were much more likely to be involved in learning programmes if they enjoyed good material circumstances (including regular, secure incomes), greater social mobility, and cultural familiarity (Hédoux, 1982; McGivney, 1990, p. 13). In particular, as McGivney put it, Hédoux had found that 'educational participation was strongly connected with the extent of an individual's integration into community life', with participants taking a much more active role than non-participants, encompassing a broader range of organisational contexts, thus acquiring better ties with local leadership figures ('notables') such as teachers and local councillors (McGivney, 1990, p. 13). McGivney also cited a second study by the same author, this time of non-participant groups ('non-publics de la formation d'adultes'), whom Hédoux had divided into two groups: while the first group knew about the opportunities and thought well of them, they preferred not to take part themselves; the second group, largely made up of people with very limited social connections, had little or no knowledge of the opportunities (Hédoux, 1981; McGivney, 1990, pp. 15–6).

In 1990, McGivney concluded that Hédoux was right to see participation in education as a differentiating factor within the working-class population (McGivney, 1990, p. 13). Her treatment of the relationship between civic engagement and adult learning, however, was relatively brief. Partly this was because Hédoux had found that civic engagement was only one of a number of factors that appeared to explain patterns of participation within the manual working class; others included such factors as being the subject of 'downward intergenerational mobility' or having a spouse who was in work. Nevertheless, Hédoux's work was important, not least in discovering that different types of civic engagement appeared to have different consequences for education. People who took part in 'traditional societies' such as sports groups, patriotic clubs and musical ensembles were no more likely to join an education activity than were those who did not join civic groups at all. By contrast, Hédoux found that people who joined 'socio-cultural associations' such as consumer movements, political parties and youth clubs, were more likely to take part in education. He also found a strong tie between educational participation and involvement in communal cultural practices such as fêtes and May Day rallies (Hédoux, 1982, pp. 265–7). Perhaps we should add that in northern French mining regions during the 1970s and 1980s, many such activities were organised by the Communist Party and its affiliated institutions, such as the daily paper *L'Humanité*.

Given the political atmosphere in Britain at the time when McGivney was writing, it is perhaps understandable that she did not draw attention to the more political dimension of civic engagement, but contented herself with Hédoux's description of educational participants as members of an 'active social minority' (McGivney, 1990, p. 13; Hédoux, 1982, p. 255). Moreover, the mining community itself was in a state of flux at the time that Hédoux was carrying out his fieldwork; the 'old militants' were retiring in large numbers during the 1970s, and a number of interviewees expressed the belief that their world was falling apart; even in the bars, old pastimes like darts were giving way to table football and other standardised activities. For those older activists, pit closures and the decline of communist politics were closely intertwined (Dubar, Guyot and Hédoux, 1982, pp. 413–23).

To some extent, then, the forms of civic engagement that Hédoux had described were passing into the past, and it was not at all clear that Communist-led festivals and rallies had much relevance to the post-industrial landscape that was the context for McGivney's own work. Moreover, Hédoux was clearly describing a strongly patriarchal world, dominated culturally by high levels of male unionised employment; women were largely absent from Hédoux's account, and it is doubtful that women in French mining districts had as much to regret as the men with the passing of old civic associations and unions that had dominated so much cultural and social activity in the past.

So Hédoux's work had important limitations, which McGivney in 1990 chose to ignore. However, this is an issue to which she has returned in a series of studies of participation in learning. In her studies of male participation in education and training, for instance, McGivney summarised a number of studies which had found that men generally tend to have fewer social ties and engage less in public civic activity than women, arguing that this 'reduces their likelihood of engaging in learning' (McGivney, 2004, p. 68). Typically, McGivney reported, men's social bonds do not allow for deep trust, yet neither are their networks of the extended and non-familial kind that allows for a broader collective identification (McGivney, 2004, pp. 70–1). These insights into a gender perspective on civic engagement and adult learning have not yet been followed up empirically, though there is a small amount of theoretical and critical commentary which touches on this subject, usually from a feminist standpoint (e.g. Blaxter and Hughes, 2000).

Only from the later 1990s was any serious research conducted into the relationship between adult learning and civic engagement. Hédoux's work, although pathbreaking, was limited, and McGivney's original insights were not built on as systematically as they might have been. Although her writing on this subject has been cited – as has Hédoux's, sometimes without any mention of McGivney's text – it was not generally subjected to empirical scrutiny. Ironically, the most detailed study of civic engagement and adult learning undertaken in the UK – the path-breaking large-scale study of learning in voluntary organisations led by Konrad Elsdon in the early 1990s – chose not to address the causal nature of the relationship, nor did it explicitly consider theoretical aspects of the learning promoted through volunteering (Elsdon, Reynolds and Stewart, 1995). Rather, the Elsdon study reflected a wider interest in the 1980s and early 1990s in developing closer relations between adult education providers and the voluntary sector. That this has changed is partly a consequence of a much more positive relationship between policy makers and the research community than existed for most of the 1980s and 1990s. As a result, recent studies of the wider benefits of learning, and of the relationships between social capital/networks and informal learning, are encouraging a more cautious understanding of the evidence, and a more selective application of lessons for policy and practice.

The social capital debate has proven to be a rich seam for researchers into adult learning. Briefly, social capital can be defined as the resources people derive from their connections with others. More precisely, it suggests that networks and ties, underpinned by a shared set of values, give rise to trust and reciprocity, which then enable people to co-operate more effectively with each other (Field, 2003). This theory is of interest to adult learning researchers for a number of reasons. First, and most basic, the theory of social capital is fundamentally about learning. At its heart, the theory clearly implies that people learn how to co-operate through exposure to a series of experiences; it also rests on the assumption that people who co-operate successfully with others will subsequently develop a trusting outlook towards those others, and will learn that reciprocity is a sensible way of behaving. Strangely, then, the social capital debate has been conducted with barely any attention so far to the ways in which this learning takes place. This is clearly an important agenda for future research, which will be likely to draw on existing social theories of learning, as well as on the insights of related studies into informal, experiential and workplace learning. The adult learning research community has much to offer this future agenda.

Second, theories of social capital have opened up important new avenues of enquiry. Embedded in ideas of a learning society are suggestions that our social arrangements and our learning are closely interrelated; the possibility must exist that some types of social arrangement are more favourable to lifelong learning than others. Social capital offers one way of conceptualising these issues, allowing us to operationalise them for purposes of research and – I would hope – practice. Of course, the concept is a broad one, encompassing everyday and intimate ties as well as the pubic and civic ties of organisational life; it can also refer to imagined ties, such as those which bind together people who may have no direct contact with one another (Quinn, 2005). But in drawing attention to the ways in which social networks serve as a resource, the concept enables us to look at people's involvement in learning in new ways.

People's social capital is itself a resource for their learning. A number of scholars have studied this aspect of the association between social capital and adult learning (e.g. La Valle and Blake, 2001; Ferlander, 2003; Field, 2006b; Quinn, 2005; Strawn, 2002). Their findings suggest that people's networks certainly influence their capacity for accessing new information, skills and ideas. Further, the nature of people's networks can also determine the variety of new knowledge and techniques to which people are exposed; crudely put, the more heterogeneous the ties, the greater the variety of knowledge and techniques, and therefore the greater the probability that one's existing knowledge and skills will be supplemented. There is also some evidence that high trust relationships are more likely to lead to the sharing of hot information, but they are also less likely to involve heterogeneity. People's social relations also appear to influence their attitudes towards education and training at different stages of the life span. Again, crudely summarised, people involved in civic activities of most kinds are more likely to look favourably on learning in adult life than people involved in more individualistic lifestyles or with fewer connections. There is also abundant evidence that people derive other forms of support from their social ties which help them learn (and to persist in learning), as well as evidence that some kinds of ties can hold learners back. This may be the case with some of the social ties that are often thought typical of men, particularly working-class men, for example (McGivney, 2004). So on this side of the equation, the evidence is complex, but it certainly confirms that social relationships matter, and on balance it suggests that social capital tends to promote learning more often than not.

On the other side of the equation, it is now absolutely unarguable that adult learning influences people's social connections. The most compelling evidence of this, without a doubt, comes from the research programme of the Wider Benefits of Learning Research Centre at the University of London (www.learningbenefits.net). This work draws on longitudinal analyses of cohort data, which show changes in individuals' behaviour and attitudes over time, and on a large body of individual cases based on detailed interviews, in a systematic attempt to examine how learning affects people's health, family lives and participation in civic life, revealing the downsides of education as well as the benefits. The overall findings for the impact of adult learning are generally very impressive ones (Schuller *et al*, 2004). More specifically, the research demonstrated that adult learning made a generally positive contribution to people's social capital. In particular, adult learning leads to stronger communities (albeit not always in ways that policy-makers might expect). Adult learning also appears to produce attitudinal effects on people's social relationships and outlook, including an increasing level of concern about wider social issues such as the environment and a greater willingness to take work, alongside reducing levels of racism and cynicism; by contrast, and counter perhaps to anecdotal common sense, it appears to have little impact on traditional family values (Preston and Feinstein, 2004). However, these effects are both limited in extent and rather complicated, and they can also be relatively short term. They might also be seen as potentially controversial, so all in all the implications for policy and practice may not be entirely straightforward.

The research field has, then, moved on significantly since *Education's for Other People* first saw the light of day. In the UK, research into adult learning generally has benefited from a considerable injection of new resources since the mid-1990s; particularly influential have been the Department for Education and Skills in England (whose research budget supported the Wider Benefits Centre) and the Economic and Social Research Council (whose activities since the mid-1990s have included the Learning Society Programme and the Teaching and Learning Research Programme). In an interesting echo of Hédoux's findings, a secondary analysis of oral history transcripts in South Wales, undertaken as part of the ESRC's Learning Society programme, demonstrated a dramatic decline after the 1960s in the level of informal learning associated with involvement in local politics (Gorard, Fevre and Rees, 1999, p. 441). However, the South Wales study also reported steep falls in informal learning associated with many hobbies, suggesting that political engagement may not have had the primacy that Hédoux gave it in his own work. The South Wales study also demonstrated the lasting legacy of family background upon subsequent participation in learning in adult life (Gorard, Rees and Fevre, 1999).

As well as benefiting from new public support, the existing specialised adult learning research community has been joined by researchers from neighbouring fields. Social scientists specialising in education were responsible for the South Wales study cited above. New and highly significant work has also come from social scientists in other fields, such as the Centre for Labour Market Studies at Leicester University, who have challenged and developed the tradition of participation analyses, and are using survey data to analyse informal workplace learning (Felstead *et al*, 2005). Among other findings, the CLMS research has tended to emphasise the importance of the workplace as an independent influence upon participation; workplace relationships, and particularly those involving line managers, appear to provide an important learning resource.

Research into civic engagement and adult learning, then, has been influenced very significantly by a number of developments since McGivney first drew Hédoux's work to our attention (Biesta, 2005). In so far as these developments have encouraged new work on civic and adult learning, though, the subsequent findings have largely tended to confirm Hédoux's initial insights. In summary, they tend to confirm that social relationships matter, and civic engagement is an important aspect of social relationships; however, some types of social relationship (and civic engagement) are more likely to promote organised learning and/or informal learning than others. The South Wales study has also suggested that some opportunities for informal learning have disappeared for the manual worker communities typified by the coal-mining industry. However, considerable bodies of research have also gone beyond the limitations of Hédoux's work, including notably McGivney's own important subsequent work on gender and participation.

Conclusion

Veronica McGivney's work, particularly *Education's for Other People*, not only reshaped the study of participation in adult learning in the UK. It also helped to consolidate its central place in the wider field of lifelong learning research and scholarship, according it a set of concerns and key questions that are particularly distinctive to this important tradition of UK adult education research. This chapter has concentrated particularly on how research into the dual influences of active citizenship and adult learning has developed since McGivney drew our attention to the empirical investigation of this link, particularly through her use of the work of Jacques Hédoux. However, this work has also shown that Hédoux's original insights, while important, were limited in a number of key respects. It can be criticised for being gender-blind; social capital can exclude as well as include, and although Hédoux described a vibrant civic learning culture among the coalminers of northern France, this was also a patriarchal culture which rested on high levels of largely invisible and unwaged female labour. Much subsequent research has explored gender, civic engagement and learning (including Jackson, 2002; McGivney, 2004). More recent research has also sought to examine newer forms of social and civic engagement, such as informal sociability or online connectivity (Ferlander and Timms, 2001), rather than pursuing Hédoux's concern with declining social and political movements. Despite these important limitations, Hédoux's early insights have provided a productive basis for further systematic research.

If Veronica McGivney were writing this chapter herself, she would now turn to a careful exploration of its implications for policy and practice. This can be done fairly briefly. Very broadly, there is now a convincing body of evidence which supports the view that people's level of social capital relates to their participation in learning, independent of other facts such as their age, class and prior education. However, the relationship between social capital and participation in learning is described by most researchers as a complex one, and the conclusions of policy and practice are therefore not simple and straightforward. It is probably safe to conclude that this evidence confirms what we already know about the importance of community-based learning and work-based learning as key means of widening participation; it also confirms the significance of outreach, partnership and relationship building as basic elements in any strategy for community-based learning. These lessons are already well known to practitioners, but policymakers sometimes benefit from the presence of new evidence to confirm what is already known. Some research also suggests that new technologies and new types of sociability can play an important and constructive role.

Recent research also suggests some important warnings which need to be observed. Hédoux's early insights into the differential impacts of different forms of social engagement have largely been confirmed by more recent work, which has also presented some evidence suggesting that social ties can play an exclusionary as well as inclusionary role. Policy makers and practitioners interested in using these insights to promote learning therefore need to distinguish between different forms of social capital. Even this risks over-simplification, as some types of social capital may be particularly good at promoting some kinds of learning, while other types of social capital may help promote other kinds of learning. Getting it wrong may mean that without due care, providers and policy makers may inadvertently help to reinforce existing inequalities rather than challenging and helping to overcome them. This seems to confirm the critical role played by intermediary actors who can negotiate effectively the relations between providers on the one hand and communities and learners on the other.

References

Benn, R. (1996) 'Access for adults to higher education: targeting or self-selection?' *Journal of Access Studies*, 11(2): 165–76

Benn, R. (2000) 'The genesis of active citizenship in the learning society', *Studies in the Education of Adults*, 32(2): 241–64

Biesta, G. (2005) 'The learning democracy? Adult learning and the condition of democratic citizenship', *British Journal of Sociology of Education*, 26(5): 687–703

Blaxter, L. and Hughes, C. (2000) 'Social capital: a critique', in J. Thompson (ed) *Stretching the Academy: The Politics and Practice of Widening Participation in Higher Education*, Leicester: National Institute of Adult Continuing Education

Dubar, C., Guyot, G. and Hédoux, J. (1982) 'Sociabilité minière et changement social à Sallaumines, Noyelles-sous-Lens, 1900–1980', *Revue du Nord*, 64: 365–463

Edwards, R. (1997) *Changing Places? Flexibility, Lifelong Learning and a Learning Society*, London: Routledge

Elsdon, K. T., Reynolds, J. and Stewart, S. (1995) *Voluntary Organisations: Citizenship, Learning and Change*, Leicester: National Institute of Adult Continuing Education

Felstead, A., Fuller, A., Unwin, L., Ashton, D., Butler, P. and Lee, T. (2005) 'Surveying the scene: learning metaphors, survey design and the workplace context', *Journal of Education and Work*, 19(4): 359–83

Ferlander, S. (2003) *The Internet, Social Capital and Local Community*, Ph. D. Thesis, University of Stirling

Ferlander, S. and Timms, D. (2001) 'Local nets and social capital', *Telematics and Informatics*, 18(1): 51–65

Field, J. (2003) *Social Capital*, London: Routledge

Field, J. (2006a) *Lifelong Learning and the New Educational Order*, Stoke-on-Trent: Trentham

Field, J. (2006b) *Social Networks, Innovation and Learning: Can Policies for Social Capital Promote both Economic Dynamism and Social Justice?*

Observatory PASCAL, Melbourne/Stirling, available online at www.obs-pascal.com/hottopic.php

Field, J. and Taylor, R. (1995) 'The funding and organisation of adult continuing education research in Britain: trends and prospects', *International Journal of Lifelong Education*, 14(3): 247–60

Gorard, S., Fevre, R. and Rees, G. (1999) 'The apparent decline of informal learning', *Oxford Review of Education*, 234(4): 437–54

Gorard, S., Rees, G. and Fevre, R. (1999) 'Patterns of participation in lifelong learning: do families make a difference?', *British Educational Research Journal*, 25(4): 517–532

Groombridge, B., Durant, J., Hampton, W., Woodcock, G. and Wright, A. (1982) *Adult Education and Participation*, Sheffield: Universities' Council for Adult and Continuing Education

Hédoux, J. (1981) 'Les non-publics de la formation collective', *Education Permanente*, 61: 89–105

Hédoux, J. (1982) 'Des publics et des non-publics de la formation d'adultes: l'access à l'Action Collective de Formation de Sallaumines, Noyelles-sous-Lens des 1972', *Revue Française de la Sociologie*, 23: 253–74

Jackson, S. (2002) 'Widening participation for women in lifelong learning and citizenship', *Widening Participation and Lifelong Learning*, 4(1): 5–16

La Valle, I. And Blake, M. (2001) *National Adult Learning Survey 2001*, Nottingham: Department for Education and Skills

Lovett, T. (ed.) (1988) *Radical Approaches to Adult Education: A Reader*, London: Routledge

McGivney, V. and Sims, D. (1986) *Adult Education and the Challenge of Unemployment*, Milton Keynes: Open University Press

McGivney, V. (1990) *Education's for Other People: Access to Education for Non-Participant Adults*, Leicester: National Institute of Adult Continuing Education

McGivney, V. (2004) Men *Earn, Women Learn: Bridging the gender divide in education and training*, Leicester: National Institute of Adult Continuing Education

National Institute of Adult Education (1970) *Adult Education: Adequacy of Provision*, Leicester: NIAE

Preston, J. and Feinstein, L. (2004) *Adult Education and Attitude Change, Wider Benefits of Learning Research Report*, Number 11, London: Institute of Education

Quinn, J. (2005) 'Belonging in a learning community: the re-imagined university and imagined social capital', *Studies in the Education of Adults*, 37(1): 4–17

Ranson, S. (ed.) (1998) *Inside the Learning Society*, London: Cassell

Schuller, T., Preston, J., Hammond, C., Bassett-Grundy, A. and Bynner, J. (2004) *The Benefits of Learning: The Impact of Education on Health, Family Life and Social Capital*, London: Routledge Falmer

Thompson, J. (ed.) (1980) *Adult Education for a Change*, London: Hutchinson

Thompson, J. (1983) *Learning Liberation: Women's Response to Men's Education*, Beckenham: Croom Helm

Notes

[1] In 1990, my view of adult education research was largely negative. McGivney was one of a number of writers who showed me that adult learning could be studied rigorously, without losing sight of its purpose. It probably helped me, and perhaps others, that *Education's for Other People* was based on work carried out with financial support from the Economic and Social Research Council.

Bibliography

Veronica McGivney

Books and reports

(1980) 'Europe and the Third World', *Exploring Europe series*, Sussex European Research Centre in collaboration with BBC Schools Radio, Falmer, Sussex

(1981) *Europe in the School: Report of the UK Research Project for DG12* Sussex European Research Centre, Falmer, Sussex

(1982) *European Dimensions in the 10–16 Curriculum*, Sussex European Research Centre and the British Council

(1985) *Working Together: Voluntary/Statutory Relationships in the Education of Adults*, Leicester: NIACE/ UDACE

(1990) *Education's for Other People: Access to Education for Non-Participant Adults*, Leicester: NIACE.

(1991) *Childcare: A Guide to Organisations, Research and Campaigns Concerned with Day Care Provision and Facilities for Children*, Leicester: REPLAN.

(1992) *Motivating Unemployed Adults to Undertake Education and Training: Some British and other European Findings*, Leicester: NIACE/REPLAN

(1992) *The Women's Education Project in Northern Ireland*, Belfast: Women's Education Project

(1992) *Tracking Adult Learning Routes: Learners' Starting Points and*

172

Progression to Further Education and Training, Leicester: NIACE

(1992) *Opening Colleges to Adult Learners*, Leicester: NIACE

(1993) *Women, Education and Training: Barriers to Access, Informal Starting Points and Progression Routes*, Leicester: NIACE

(1994) *Adult Learning Pathways: A Case Study in the Taff Ely District Funded by Mid Glamorgan TEC and Welsh Office: Final Report*, Cardiff: NIACE Cymru

(1994) *Wasted Potential: Training and Career Progression for Part-Time and Temporary Workers*, Leicester: NIACE.

(1994) *Identifying the Use of Skills Gained on Adult Continuing Education and Training Courses Provided by Gloucestershire Local Education Authority – Full Report*, Gloucestershire: ACET

(1994) *Economic Development*, Summary Report 1, Gloucestershire: ACET

(1994) *Social and Personal Benefits: the Implications for Social Services*, Summary Report 2, Gloucestershire: ACET

(1994) *Educational Progression*, Summary Report 3, Gloucestershire: ACET

(1994) *Developing the Confident Learner: The Contribution of Adult Education to a Culture of Lifetime Learning*, Summary Report 4, Gloucestershire: ACET

(1995) *Women Returners: Their Educational Needs and Attitudes: A Study for the Heart of England Training and Enterprise Council*, Oxford: Heart of England TEC

(1996) *An Evaluation of the Heart of England TEC Programme of New Provision for Women Returners: A Report for the Heart of England TEC*, Oxford: Heart of England TEC

(1996, revised edition 2003) *Staying or Leaving the Course: Non Completion and Retention of Mature Students in Further and Higher Education*, Leicester: NIACE

(1997) *Develop the Worker, Develop the Business: A Guide for Smaller Businesses*, Leicester : NIACE

(1998) *Adults Learning in Pre-Schools*, Leicester: NIACE and London: Pre-school Learning Alliance

(1999) *Returning Women: Their Education and Training Choices and Needs*, Leicester: NIACE

(1999) *Informal Learning in the Community: A Trigger for Change and Development*, Leicester: NIACE

(1999) *Excluded Men: Men who are Missing from Education and Training*, Leicester: NIACE

(2000) *Recovering Outreach: Concepts, Issues and Practices*, Leicester: NIACE

(2000) *The Contribution of Pre-Schools to the Community: A Research Study on the Role of Pre-Schools in Tackling Social Exclusion*, London: Pre-School Learning Alliance

(2000) *Working with Excluded Groups: Guidance on Good Practice for Providers and Policy-Makers in Working with Groups Under-Represented in Adult Learning: Based on the Oxfordshire Widening Participation Project*, Leicester: NIACE/Oxfordshire Strategic Partnership

(2001) *Fixing or Changing the Pattern? Reflections on Widening Adult Participation in Learning*, Leicester: NIACE

(2002) *A Question of Value: Achievement and Progression in Adult Learning: A Discussion Paper*, Leicester: NIACE

(2002) *Spreading the Word: Reaching Out to New Learners*, Leicester: NIACE

(2003) *Adult Learning Pathways: Through-Routes or Cul-De-Sacs?*, Leicester: NIACE

(2004) *Adult Learning at a Glance: The UK Context, Facts and Figures*, Vol. 1, Leicester: NIACE

(2004) *The Impact of Pre-Schools in the Community: A Follow-Up Study*, London: Pre-school Learning Alliance

(2004) *Men Earn, Women Learn: Bridging the Gender Divide in Education and Training*, Leicester: NIACE

(2005) *Keeping the Options Open: The Importance of Maintaining a Broad and Flexible Curriculum Offer for Adults: A Discussion Paper*, Leicester: NIACE

(2006) *Adult Learning at a Glance: The UK Context, Facts and Figures*, Vol. 2, Leicester: NIACE

Joint publications

Champney, J., Davey, M., Lawrence, S., McGivney, V., McGuire, P., Quilter, R., Summers, J., Meyer, S. and Armstrong, A. (2005) *Breaking Down the Barriers: Success in Widening Participation: A Toolkit Approach*, London: LSDA

Charnley, A.H. and McGivney, V. (1986), *Indicators of Fee Levels Charged to Part-Time Adult Students by Local Education Authorities*, Leicester: NIACE

Charnley, A.H. and McGivney, V. (1987), *Indicators of Fee Levels Charged to Part-Time Adult Students by Local Education Authorities: NIACE Fee Survey, 1986-87*, Leicester: NIACE

Charnley, A. H. and McGivney, V. (1988) *NIACE Fee Survey: Indicators of Fee Levels Charged to Part-Time Adult Students by Local Education Authorities*, Leicester: NIACE

Charnley, A.H., McGivney, V. and Sims, D. (1985) *Education for the Adult Unemployed: Some Responses*, Leicester: NIACE

Charnley, A.H., McGivney, V. and Withnall, A. (1986) *Care in the Community: Adult Continuing Education and Joint Finance*, Leicester: NIACE

Coats, M. and McGivney, V. (1987) *Women and Access to Education and Training in Britain*, an explanatory document, EBAE/REPLAN

Goodson, I. and McGivney, V. (1985), *European Dimensions and the Secondary School Curriculum*, London, Philadelphia: Falmer Press

McCaffery, J. and McGivney V. (1988) *Linking Women's Groups: A Report on an Exploratory Visit to KENYA*, London: The British Council

McGivney, V. and Charnley, A.H. (1987) *Replan Regional Staff Development Programmes, 1985/86: A Research Report* Leicester: NIACE

McGivney, V. and Murray, F. (1991) *Adult Education in Development: Methods and Approaches from Changing Societies*, Leicester: NIACE and the British Council

McGivney, V. and Sims, D. (1986) *Adult Education and the Challenge of Unemployment*, Milton Keynes: Open University Press

McGivney, V. and Thomson, A, (1995) *Foundation Training: Responding to Labour Market Change*: *A Report for Coventry City Council City Development Directorate*, Coventry: Coventry City Council

McGivney, V., Thompson J. and Turner, C. (2004) *Community Leadership Training Pilots*: *Final Report*, Leicester: NIACE/DfES

McNair, S., Cara, S., McGivney, V., Raybould, F., Soulsby, J., Thomson, A. and Vaughan, M. (1999) *Non-Award Bearing Continuing Education: An Evaluation of the HEFCE Programme 1995–1998*, Bristol: HEFCE

Moore, R., McGivney, V. and Alexandrou, A. (1993) *Evaluation Survey into Participation and Non-Participation in the Ford Employee Development Programme (EDAP)*, Oxford: Trade Union Research Unit, Ruskin College

Withnall, A., McGivney, V., Soulsby, J. (2004), *Older People Learning: Myths and Realities*, Leicester: NIACE and DfES

Winkless, C. and McGivney, V. (1989) *Indicators of Fee Levels Charged to Adult Students by Local Education Authorities, 1988–89*, Leicester: NIACE

Winkless, C. and McGivney, V. (1992). *NIACE Fee Survey 1991-92: Indicators of Fee Levels Charged to Part-Time Adult Students by Local Education Authorities and Colleges*, Leicester: NIACE

Chapters

(1991) 'Taller sobre la formacion basica para mujeres' in European Bureau of Adult Education (ed), *Educaion de Base para Mujeres en EUROPA*, Brussels: European Bureau of Adult Education

(1994) 'Patterns of participation and non participation' in Crawford, M., Edwards, R. and Kydd, L. (eds), *Learning through Life: Education and Training beyond School*, Milton Keynes: Open University Press

(1998) 'Guidance and retention of mature students in further and higher education', in *Taking Issue: Debates in Guidance and Counselling in Learning,* Milton Keynes: Open University Press/Routledge

(2002) 'Informal learning in the UK' in Taylor, S. and Cameron, C. (eds) *Attracting New Learners: International Evidence and Practice.* London: LSDA

(2003) 'Match or mismatch: do the findings reflect the qualitative evidence?' in Sargant, N. and Aldridge, F. (eds) *Adult Learning and Social Division: A Persistent Pattern: Volume 2: Issues Arising from the NIACE Survey on Adult Participation in Learning 2002*, Leicester: NIACE

(2006) 'Attracting new groups into learning: lessons from research in England' in Chapman, J., Cartwright, P. and McGilp, J. (eds), *Lifelong Learning: Participation and Equity*, Australian Catholic University and Netherlands: Springer Press

(2006) 'Informal learning: the challenge for research' in Edwards, Gallagher J. and Whittaker S, *Learning outside the Academy: International Research Perspectives on Lifelong Learning*, London and New York: Routledge

Journal Articles

Ecclestone, K. and McGivney, V. (2005) 'Are adult educators obsessed with developing self-esteem?', *Adults Learning*, 16(5): 8–13

McGivney V. (1980) 'Europe in the curriculum', *Journal of the Modern Studies Association*, Spring 1980

McGivney V. (1980) 'Europe in the school', *Teaching about Europe*, No. 3. Summer 1980

McGivney, V. (1990). 'Non-participant adult groups: recruitment and programme development', *Adults Learning*, 1(6): 156–158

McGivney, V. (1991). 'Opening colleges to adult learners', *Adults Learning*, 2(10): 289–292

McGivney, V. (1991). 'Come in, the door is open: results of a NIACE project on making colleges more attractive to adult learners', *Education*, 178(9): 167–168

McGivney, V. (1991) 'Women in the USSR', *Working with Women*, REPLAN, Spring 1991

McGivney, V. (1991) 'Adult education in development', *Adults Learning*, 3(4): 95

McGivney, V. (1992) 'Tracking adult learning routes: adult learners' starting points and progression', *Adults Learning*, 3(6): 140–142

McGivney, V. (1992) 'Women and vocational training: an overview'. *Adults Learning*, 3(10): 260–264

McGivney, V. (1994) 'Women, education and training', *Adults Learning*, 5(5): 118–120

McGivney, V. (1994) 'Part-time training', *Training Tomorrow*, July 1994: 17–19

McGivney, V. (1994). 'Part-time workers and the achievement of the National Targets for Education and Training', *Adults Learning*, 6(1): 38–40

McGivney, V. (1995). 'Skills, knowledge and economic outcomes: a pilot study of adult learners in Gloucestershire', *Adults Learning*, 6(6): 172–175

McGivney, V. (1996). 'Staying or leaving the course: non completion and retention', *Adults Learning*, 7(6): 133–135

McGivney, V. (1997) 'The learning and other outcomes for parents involved in pre-schools', *Adults Learning*, 8(5): 124–127

McGivney, V. (1998) 'Life begins at pre-school', *Guardian Education*, 19th May 1998

McGivney, V. (2000). 'Informal learning and bridging the class divide in educational participation'. *Rising East: The Journal of East London Studies: Special Issue: Lifelong Learning and East London in association with the University of East London's Festival of Lifelong Learning*. London: Lawrence & Wishart

McGivney, V. (2000) 'Recovering outreach', *Adults Learning*, 12(3): 7–9

McGivney, V. (2000) 'Sweeping the boards or sweeping the floors?', *Adults Learning*, 11(7): 27

McGivney, V. (2001) 'Informal learning: a neglected species', *Scottish Journal of Adult and Continuing Education*, 7(2): 101–108

McGivney, V. (2001) 'Why is education still for "other people"?', *Adults Learning*, 1(3): 14–16

McGivney, V. (2003). 'It's easier to define adult and community learning by saying what it is not!', *Adult Learning & Skills*, 1: 4–5

McGivney, V. (2003) 'Widening participation and progression: neither linear nor straightforward', *Adult Learning & Skills*, 2: 4–5

McGivney, V. (2004) 'Understanding persistence in adult learning', *Open Learning: The Journal of Open and Distance Learning*, 19(1): 33–46

McGivney, V. (2005) 'Death by a thousand cuts', *Adults Learning*, 17(4): 8–11

McGivney, V. (2006) 'It was 20 years ago today . . .', *Adults Learning*, 17(6): 8–10

McGivney, V. and Bateson, B. (1991) 'Childcare: the continuing debate', *Adults Learning*, 2(7): 203–204

McGivney, V. and McCaffery, J. (1991) 'Are you opening doors to women? A checklist of good practice', *Adults Learning*, 2(7)

Index

Index

Index